A Desert Transformed

Discovering God's joy and presence
in the wilderness seasons of life

A 40 day devotional

TRACY WILLIAMSON

RIVER
PUBLISHING

River Publishing & Media Ltd
info@river-publishing.co.uk
www.river-publishing.co.uk

ISBN 978-1-908393-90-6
Printed in the UK

Contents

What Others Are Saying...

Tracy writes with a gentle authority from the Holy Spirit. There is a quiet power to these short meditations, like a thunderstorm on mute, its energy felt rather than heard. Tracy Williamson may be hearing impaired, but she is spiritually attuned, and I sense a Voice rumbling through the gentle words of this book. Listen for that Voice as you read; it offers gentle joy in the midst of life's trials.

Sheridan Voysey
Author of *The Making of Us: Who We Can Become When Life Doesn't Go as Planned*, and *Resurrection Year: Turning Broken Dreams into New Beginnings*.

Tracy has one of the most beautiful and intimate relationships with the Lord of anyone I have ever met, so I can highly recommend this devotional. I've watched her survive many desert experiences herself, so she definitely knows what she's talking about!

Jennifer Rees Larcombe
Author, speaker and Director of Beauty from Ashes.

Take a journey with Tracy over 40 days as she shares from her life and the Bible, taking a very honest look at our experiences of anxiety, grief, fear, loneliness and depression and shows how God is always with us in those experiences and working to bring about something beautiful. With time for prayer and reflection (do have a journal to hand) this could be a life-changing read. I thoroughly recommend it.

Evelyn Smith
Director of the Canaan Christian Centre.

I first became acquainted with Tracy through a Facebook group we both belong to – the Association of Christian Writers. Since then our friendship has grown as we've communicated via email and met up a few times. I had the privilege of being a member of her Facebook Book Launch Team for her previous book, *The Father's Kiss* (a book I can highly recommend). I believe Tracy's devotional, *A Desert Transformed* will be a blessing to all who read it, particularly the many of us who have been or are going through a spiritual desert of one form or another. Tracy's love for her Father God, the close relationship she enjoys with Him, and the gift He has given her to write and share what He has placed on her heart, shines throughout this devotional. Tracy writes in such an authentic way about her own experiences that readers will easily relate to what they read. As you read her book you will receive encouragement and hope for your journey. This devotional will help you to recognise God's presence with you, His love for you and will strengthen you in your faith.

Vicki Cottingham
Author of *Dear Friend, Devotionals 1 & 2*

In *A Desert Transformed* Tracy Williamson invites us to sit a while and hear the assurances of the God who holds us in our wilderness times as well as in easier times. With Tracy's warm, prophetic voice, the rich words and reflections on Scripture in this devotional will be a blessing to the weak and weary; to those who are finding that a life of faith is not a life without pain. Readers will be greatly blessed and soothed by the gentle words of comfort Tracy offers, and the many images she paints so vividly of the Father's passionate love. This is a book which merges the ordinary with the sacred, the messy with the beautiful, and darkness with treasure. Highly recommended.

Liz Carter
Author of *Catching Contentment, How to Be Holy Satisfied*

Having lived and worked with Tracy for many years, her every day Christ-like transparency always challenges me and I am constantly learning from her selfless love and the way she gives herself wholeheartedly to serve others. So as you read, allow the water of God's Spirit to melt and soften your heart, as He did mine through two of the devotionals when I was only a quarter of the way through this book. They caused me to re-examine my attitudes and confess some hidden resentment which was narrowing my spiritual vision and hardening my heart. The readings show us how deeply the Lord understands our struggles and I believe that as you let them touch your heart, God will use them to help change and transform your desert experience.

Marilyn Baker
Singer/Songwriter and Director of MBM Trust

In this devotional Tracy Williamson invites the reader to go on a journey of discovery – about God and themselves. Recognising that we all have times of feeling like we are wandering through a wilderness, Tracy opens up Scripture and is beautifully honest about her own struggles, to show us that it is in the desert that God often does his deepest work of transformation. Tracy knows and hears God clearly and that comes across so much in her writing, which often has a prophetic element to it. I personally found this devotional incredibly helpful – each day there seemed to be something that spoke directly to my heart. I thoroughly commend this book to you.

Claire Musters
Speaker, editor and author of *Taking Off the Mask* and *An Insight into Shame*.

Acknowledgements

I am so grateful to Tim Pettingale of River Publishing for believing in me that I could bring a devotional book to birth – something I had always wanted to do, but never had the opportunity before. Thank you, Tim, for your encouragement and also for your great patience with me as I kept changing the goal posts of when I would submit the manuscript!

I would also like to thank my great friend and ministry partner Marilyn Baker for encouraging me in this work and, through your own walk with the Lord, bringing me much inspiration and challenge. Through you I have grown deeper in my own relationship with God and many of the thoughts I share in the coming readings stem from that. Thank you too for bearing with me during these months of writing and putting everything else aside, including those things we would normally do together!

Thank you for all my lovely friends, family, church and MBM supporters who have stood with me and prayed for me during these weeks of seeking the Lord and writing. Your support and prayers have empowered and enabled me.

I'd also like to thank the many devotional writers who have fed me through their writings and helped me to grow in my journey of love and faith. I am praying that this offering to the well of devotional writing may bear similar fruit in others' lives.

Thank you, dear Father, Son and Holy Spirit, for without you and your amazingly powerful Word there would be no devotional writing. You are the Alpha and Omega.

Tracy Williamson

Dedication

I would like to dedicate *A Desert Transformed* to all those who are journeying through some kind of life desert or wilderness. May you know the joy of His loving presence alongside you as you read, and His transforming love bringing you peace.

"In a desert land he found him, in a barren and howling waste. He shielded him and cared for him: he guarded him as the apple of his eye."

(Deuteronomy 32:10)

Foreword

When I was asked to write this foreword, I was at once surprised, honoured, and acutely aware of my own inadequacy. How could I write a foreword? Surely there would be better people to choose than me. The latter may well be true, but as I read *A Desert Transformed*, I realised that the book was written for precisely people like me.

I've experienced wilderness times. For example, loss of health, loss of dreams, wanting to die, feeling worthless, frustrations.

Wilderness times come, and not just to me. They probably come to you, too. Times when, for whatever reason, life is hard.

Because I have the privilege of calling Tracy Williamson a friend, I know that she has lived – and lives – through many wilderness times. You'll read about some of them in this book. And that is exactly what makes this book so real. *A Desert Transformed* is not a book written by someone for whom life has been plain sailing. This is a book written by someone who has experienced rejection, isolation and struggles yet, in those wildernesses, finds hope in God – and it's not a hope she wants to keep to herself!

These 40 readings contain personal stories, beautiful meditations and biblical examples, all of which show us that God is with us in our wildernesses – and He longs to transform us, often in ways far beyond our comprehension.

1 Corinthians 2:9 says, *"No eye has seen, no ear has heard, and no mind has imagined what God has prepared for those who love him."*

A Desert Transformed is full of gems to guide us as we walk our wildernesses, however they look, and encourages us to reach for life in all its fullness.

Read it slowly, savour it, read it again and again. Let it speak God's words into your thirsty heart and soul.

Emily Owen
Author and Speaker

Introduction

When River Publishing contacted me to ask if I'd be interested in writing a devotional, my immediate reaction was a rather nervous, "Err, yes!" I've always loved devotional writings, finding them an invaluable resource for my faith journey. Easily accessible, bite-sized portions of daily inspiration, challenge and comfort – over the years I've enjoyed and been blessed by so many rich offerings: *Word for Today, Every Day with Jesus*; devotional books by Jennifer Rees Larcombe, Joni Eareckson Tada, Joyce Meyer, Sarah Young, John Ryeland, Emily Owen… to name just a few. I loved what these authors brought me from the Word of God and gradually their writings inspired me to try myself, so I began to write a fortnightly devotional for our Ministry's website: **www.mbm-ministries.org** and became a regular contributor to BRF *Day by Day with God*, Bible reading notes for women.

But these more sporadic forms of devotional writing were one thing, doing a whole book was another, and that was where I felt nervous. What could I add that hadn't already been said? I'd had no theological training, so what could I give from the Word of God that could really inspire or comfort my readers? To put it in a nutshell, I felt inadequate for the task. Feelings of inadequacy have been the theme of my life following the difficulties of my childhood, but God has called me repeatedly to step out of my prison of fear and trust in the power of His love and grace. This time was no exception and as I prayed I knew that the Lord wanted me to go ahead.

But how was I to do it? Should I follow a theme? What kind of length should it be? River Publishing suggested I make it a 40-day devotional rather than the more cumbersome 365-day version and I felt a "yes" deep inside. As I prayed, I realised the significance of the number 40. Moses was an outcast in the desert for 40 years after murdering an Egyptian. After his encounter with God he led the Israelites through the wilderness for another 40 years. He also spent 40 days in Mount Horeb when God gave him the Ten Commandments. Elijah travelled for 40 days through the desert when he was running from Jezebel. Jesus spent 40 days in the wilderness facing testing and temptation...

As I thought of these and other instances, I sensed that God was speaking to me about the areas of our lives that can become like a wilderness: those times of grief, bereavement, loss of hope, disillusionment, anger, testing, rejection and pain. I also thought of how He loves to come alongside us and open our hearts to His deep compassion and love. Stories came to mind from the Bible of how God met with different individuals as they went through struggles and pain and brought wonderful transformation came to mind, together with His many, many promises to us throughout both Old and New Testaments of His presence, power, love, strength, purpose and forgiveness. With each insight an increasing excitement grew within me. I knew God had shown me the theme for the book – joy in the wilderness, our deserts transformed.

So here we have it – a 40-day journey into both the desert areas of our lives and into God's wonderful promises and love. I am walking the same journey as there are desert areas in my own life too, so I have included personal stories and glimpses into the ways in which God brings transformation into my woundedness. Each day's reading is complete in itself, so they don't have to be read in order, although you may find it most helpful to read them consecutively. The readings follow a rough pattern of having a title/theme, a Bible passage which I recommend you read the whole of, a quotation from that passage and then my note. Most end with a short reflection and a prayer, but some have a prophecy or a word that the Lord has given me while writing. Others are in the form of a short story or a poem. Enjoy the variations because God loves to use many ways to touch us with His love. Have your journal to hand and jot things down that inspire or move you. Every note has some suggested extra Scripture readings which I recommend you do actually read as they will make it a much fuller experience.

I do believe with all my heart that the Lord led me in this theme and that as you journey through the devotional, and through your own areas of wilderness, that He will be alongside you, speaking to you and renewing you in His wonderful love. Be blessed!

"And this is my prayer, that your love may abound more and more in knowledge and depth of insight." (Philippians 1:9)

Tracy Williamson

Day 1 – Water in the Desert

(Isaiah 43:16-21)

*"I provide water in the desert and streams in the wasteland
to give drink to my people, my chosen, the people I formed for
myself that they may proclaim my praise."*

I have a confession to make and my friends will know
immediately that this is true: I am a useless gardener. Even
indoor plants rarely survive when they are under my care. I
either water them far too much and effectively drown them
or forget to water them at all and they dry out and die. This
makes me realise how easy it is to recreate a desert in your own
home, for when it is not watered, the plant may as well be in the
Sahara! Sometimes my friends see my skeletal plants and tell
me off saying, "Trace, they were desperate for a drink!" After
they've watered and lavished some tender loving care on them,
I am amazed to see how instantly the plants are rejuvenated.
Dry, dingy leaves and stems turn green again and bounce back
to life. All it takes is one good drink and some love and that
particular desert is transformed.

This lovely passage in Isaiah 43 expresses God's desire to bring
renewal into our dry, barren places and to open up things

which seem irresolvable and impassable. A wasteland doesn't naturally have streams running through it. If it did, it would be a fertile field not a wasteland. But God is showing us that He is the God of the impossible. He wants to water the wasteland areas of our lives with the foundational truths of His love and the promises of His care and help. Truths which, if we take them deep into our hearts and minds, will have the same renewing power as that watering can renewing my houseplants. Truths that will renew and transform into new life the areas of our lives that are barren and dying. Truths such as…

…you were lovingly created by Him; He is with you; He loves you and says that you are precious and honoured in His eyes; you are called by His name and created for His glory; you are His witness and His chosen servant…

Why do we sometimes become dry and barren like a desert?

One reason is when we feel unloved and unwanted. After creating Adam God said, *"It is not good for man to be alone"* (Genesis 2:18). Feeling isolated and without hope is one of the key factors in us becoming like a desert emotionally. It doesn't matter whether we live alone or with family – we each need to feel that we matter to someone and that our lives have significance. When we hear God speaking His love-truths over us, His Spirit is given permission to *"make a way in the desert"* – to open up a fertile path of hope and joy.

On one occasion, when I was a young Christian, my identity and sense of self-worth was nil after years of struggle both at home and at school. I felt I had nothing to say that was of any importance and was a pathetic loser. A mature Christian friend encouraged me to ask God to speak to me through Isaiah 43:4 where it says, *"since you are precious and honoured in my sight and because I love you..."*. She explained that these words applied to me as much as they applied to the Israelites, because God's word is alive and powerful to heal and change us.

As I read, I suddenly remembered myself as a small girl in junior school trying to make an Easter hat in a class project. I knew how beautiful I wanted it to look but couldn't hear the teacher's instructions and it came out like a pancake. The teacher mocked it and threw it away! The Lord spoke into my heart, "I will never discard you like that teacher discarded your work. You are absolutely beautiful to me."

Reflect

May that prophetic word, "I will never discard you, you are absolutely beautiful to me" minister to you too.

Prayer

Thank you, Father, for your promise to make a way in the desert and bring streams in the wasteland. I give to you those barren places in my life and pray that you will open me up to your life-giving love and joy. Amen.

Extra Readings

Psalm 107; Exodus 3

Day 2 – Change is at the Heart of the Universe

(Ecclesiastes 3:1-14)

"There is a time for everything and a season for every activity under heaven. A time to be born and a time to die; A time to plant and a time to uproot."

What season are you experiencing at present? Are you in a time of joy and fulfilment or is it a more stressful time of loss or pain? How do you feel about change? Do you long for it or is it something you fear and avoid? When we fear change, we can dig our heels in and refuse to move forward. It's easy then to become cynical and embittered, reluctant to pray or to open ourselves to God's leading. It can turn our hearts into a desert because we are always focusing on the negatives and looking back rather than ahead with hope and trust in God's ability to work all things to the good in our lives.

A typical characteristic of deserts is their sameness. Mile after mile they continue: the same view of hot, barren sand; the same burning footsteps and extreme thirst. Sometimes our lives feel like this too, and if we are going through a difficult season it may feel like it is going to continue forever.

But God has written change into the heart of the universe. Even the desert is constantly changing beneath the surface. Sands shift, routes become obliterated and the unrelenting sameness is transformed overnight when the rains come bringing to bloom its hidden life.

In our lives too, change is constant. This morning, when I walked the dogs the air was nippy and there was a frost. Now the sun has come up and it is hot, but that early morning chill was a sign that summer is drawing to a close. As every season ends, we see evidence of the new – glimpses of what is to come. Snowdrops herald the spring, early frost the autumn. Similarly, our lives have their seasons as this passage from Ecclesiastes points out. Maybe you are beginning to notice signs of change and are feeling anxious about what may be ahead? Are you desperately trying to hold on to the "now" because it is familiar and comforting?

We all treasure aspects of our present lives – like our job or time with our children. God loves us to live in the moment, but we can get too fearful of those things changing. The disciples loved sharing in Jesus' miracles, but when He talked of suffering and dying, they were overwhelmed with grief. They completely missed the joy of His resurrection as they hadn't taken His promises on board.

God says to us all: "Every season is beautiful. It may be a very different beauty to the season you've just been in, but it will still be beautiful because I will be with you in it. I will open your eyes to new signs of my love and grace. It will be a means of you drawing closer to me and growing stronger in your faith, so don't be afraid, but even now look for and treasure the glimpses I will give you of what is to come and the promise of my presence with you."

Reflect

In Genesis 1 the very emptiness of the universe was transformed as God spoke life into it. The Spirit of God was hovering over the surface of the waters, ready to bring beauty in response to His word. He is ready to bring new beauty in your life too. Spend time quietly offering Him any barren areas of your life and tell Him you are willing to step into the changes of a new season.

Prayer

Lord, thank you that every season of my life is beautiful because you are with me in it. Forgive me for fearing change and looking back all the time. Help me to trust and to see with your eyes. Amen.

Extra Readings

Luke 24:13-35; Psalm 103:1-14

Day 3 – I Thirst

(John 4:7 & John 19:28-29)

"Jesus said 'I thirst.'"

Are you thirsty?

I am privileged to live somewhere that has water on tap, but other parts of the world have very little water and people have to keep digging new wells as old ones dry up.

Thirst is a primal need. We cannot survive physically without water and when we feel thirsty, the relief we experience from drinking is profound. Thirst and God's power to quench it, is expressed throughout the Bible, especially when the Israelites were wandering in the wilderness for forty years. God provided miraculously for them, even causing a stream to erupt out of a rock when Moses struck it with his staff (Numbers 20:11).

Only God could do that and only God can reach our inner thirst, which goes deeper even than our physical need. We thirst for meaning in life – for fulfilment, love, beauty, hope, truth and ultimately God Himself. Only God can truly satisfy our longing. As Jesus cried out, *"Let anyone who is thirsty come to me and drink. Whoever believes in me, as Scripture has said, rivers of living water will flow from within them"* (John 7:37).

Are you thirsty?

Do you know what your heart is aching for?

Jesus longs to meet that need and it was that very heartache that He carried to the cross, where His words, "I thirst" were some of His last. He who offered living water to all, knew the deepest thirst possible. His agonising death, His willingness to carry our thirst that we might be satisfied, and ultimately His passionate longing for us to receive His love, were all enshrined in those words.

As I reflected on this and the occasion when Jesus asked the Samaritan woman for a drink (John 4:4–26), the following prophetic poem came to me:

Please could you give me a drink?
Won't you look into my face?
Let down your guard of distance,
Look child, my beloved one,
Can you not see,
I thirst.

I thirst for love of you.
You know your own pain
And shield your face from me,
Lest you be hurt yet again.
I gaze on you, see your heartache,
The scars that hurt you deep within,
And my heart aches with love for you.

But child, will you not look
And see how, in my own scars,
I bear your every wound, every sin?
Child, I love you,
Will you not come give me a drink?
"What drink can I give you?"
I hear you cry.

Do you not know, child?
I thirst for you, for your love,
For you to be with me
As I love to be with you.
I thirst to share my heart with you,
For you to share yours with me.
To open wide the door of wonder
In your heart, mind and soul.

Child, it is I, who stands at that door,
Yes, I who speak to you am He.
And I long to be with you,
And for you to be with me.
I see a dawning of hope in your eyes
But then you cry "But what can *I* give *you*?
I am empty, my love is so small.
I've failed and I don't know how to be."

I reach out my arms to you,
Child, I know, I know all.
Give me the drink of your very emptiness
And I will give you my streams of love,
Love welling up to eternity.

I gaze at you with all the longing of my heart,
That you will see I am the answer
To all the longing of yours.

Child, beloved one, will you give me a drink?
And with a joy that bursts from my very core
I see you come and sit at my knee
And there you offer your drink to me.

Prayer

Thank you, with all my heart that you satisfy my thirst completely. Thank you that you died on the cross that I might know the depths of your love and that my love for you brings joy to your heart too. I give you all my emptiness and shame, Lord, and ask that you will fill that deep inner thirst with your promised streams of living water. Amen.

Extra Readings

Mark 10:17-22; Psalm 107:35

Day 4 – From Despair to Joy

(Luke 8:42-48)

*"She came trembling and fell at his feet. In the presence of all
the people she told why she had touched him and how she had
been instantly healed. Then he said to her: 'Daughter your faith
has healed you. Go in peace.'"*

Are you feeling weary today? May you know the Father
wrapping you with His love and tending you with loving
kindness. Let this story of the sick woman who received a
wonderful touch from Jesus bring you deep comfort.

Chronic illness is one of the most debilitating things we can
ever contend with. The cumulative effect of physical pain,
weakness, lack of sleep, extreme weariness and depression
wear us down and make life a battle to survive rather than a
joyful adventure.

Some things feel unendurable and getting out of that hard
place seems impossible – a desert without end. As Psalm 42:3
describes so graphically,

*"My tears have been my food day and night, while people say to
me all day long, 'Where is your God?'"*

Are you in that desert of hopelessness today?

Remember, Jesus is our living hope and always desires to turn around the impossible and pour joy into our lives. Nothing is too difficult for Him.

This woman had been bleeding for twelve years and had spent all her money seeking healing. Despite this, her condition was worse and its nature meant that she could never ask for help because she was ceremonially unclean. People shunned her lest they become unclean too. How deep her emotional pain must have been, to be so isolated with no hope of anything changing.

But when all hope seems to be stripped away, God prompts us to throw ourselves on His mercy. Some of the reports circulating about the miracles Jesus was doing must have reached the woman's ears and birthed something new; a tiny flame of hope that Jesus would help her. That if she could just push through that crowd and touch Jesus' cloak, she would be healed.

Prior to this, there is no mention in Scripture of someone being healed by touching Jesus' robe, so what gave her this idea? I believe it was divine revelation through the Holy Spirit. When we consciously enter God's presence and open ourselves to His voice, true hope is born.

She chose to act on His prompting, pushed her fears and pain aside and began to press forward through the crowd. The Bible says that *"when she touched the edge of His cloak her bleeding immediately stopped."* How incredible!

But Jesus made a choice to minister to her secret longing for love and affirmation too. He called her out and said to her, *"Daughter, your faith has healed you. Go in peace."* That name *"daughter"* was so what she needed to hear. She who had been forced outside the community was now being told that she belonged.

Jesus never leaves us in our brokenness and that was why He wanted the woman to say what she had done. It can be scary to make ourselves vulnerable in front of others, to admit that we have needs. But Jesus loves us too much to let us stay hidden. Listen for His call of love. Come out from your hiding place. He wants to affirm you and call you "Daughter" or "Son". That woman was transformed by His choice to love her into wholeness. Let Him love you into wholeness too.

Prayer

Thank you, Lord Jesus, for the hope you offer me. Thank you that with your help I can find new strength to press through all the obstacles and reach out to you with my need. Thank you that you are so willing to answer in ways that are beyond what I can ever imagine. Thank you that you always love me into wholeness. Lord, here I am. Amen.

Extra Readings

Psalm 103:1-5; Ephesians 1:3-8

Day 5 – An Everlasting Love

(Jeremiah 31:3-14)

"The Lord appeared to us in the past, saying: 'I have loved you with an everlasting love; I have drawn you with unfailing kindness.'"

Have you ever fallen in love?

Maybe you are happily living with your life partner now and, if so, that is wonderful. But many of us have experienced the pain of a broken relationship or a friendship that has gone sour and the idea of a forever kind of love feels like a disappointing myth.

I fell in love big time when I was in my first year at college. Tim was loving and extrovert. I was shy and loved that he could take the lead in all social situations. I never thought he would even notice a quiet little mouse like me, but he did and when he asked me out, I felt all my dreams were coming true at once! But nearly 37 years on I am still single and as much as I loved Tim, that particular dream was never to be fulfilled. It was no one's fault; it just wasn't right. But even when something isn't right, its loss can create an arid area in our hearts – a feeling of unfulfilled longing. It is into this particular area that God speaks when He says to us,

"I have loved you with an everlasting love."

What is God saying through these words?

Can they change the loss of our hopes into an oasis of peace? *"I have loved you..."* says the Lord. The phrasing speaks of a love that reaches back to the very beginning of Creation. He didn't just love us from the time we became Christians, but always.

When you love someone, you feel emotionally connected to them even when you're not together. If they walk into a crowded room, your whole focus will be on them and theirs on you. Love singles that person out and draws them into your heart. So, God is saying,

"I have always loved you and always will love you. I will never give up on you. Don't imagine you can just walk away from me, for I am in you and you are in me. I will never leave or forsake you. You cannot disappoint me for I already know everything about you and still love you. Your actions may grieve me at times, but my forgiveness is an ever-flowing river. I am always seeking to show you the riches of my lovingkindness. You will always be my focus, my number one."

Does that word encourage you? One thing it brought home to me is how persistent God's love is. Some people get offended if they can't see their friends regularly, but true friendship stays true, even if you don't see a person for several years.

Recently, I went to stay with some dear friends from the past. I feared we might all have moved on too much to still be friends, but we all picked up from where we'd left off. We shared and laughed together; we were relaxed. It didn't matter that we hadn't been in touch. The friendship was just the same and I felt so happy and enriched to have that time together.

Jesus is that same true friend who never takes offence and is committed to us *forever*. Do you worry sometimes that you haven't made enough time for prayer or reading the Bible? Do you withdraw from Him, thinking that He must have already withdrawn from you because you've failed Him yet again?

Jesus says:

"You are my beloved friend and I love you with an 'everlasting' love. Open the door of your heart afresh to me today and I will come and share a meal with you, and we can enjoy being together again. We can chat, laugh and even cry together. To be with you is my greatest joy and always will be."

Extra Readings

John 15

Day 6 – In the Throes of Resentment

(Luke 10:38-41)

"Lord, don't you care that my sister has left me to do the work by myself? Tell her to help me!"

Martha's story describes the kind of wilderness any of us can enter. You don't need to have had a big crisis; this wilderness can creep up inside you because of an inward struggle or a hurtful conflict. But if it's not dealt with it can become like quicksand, sucking you down until, like Martha, you find yourself in the throes of resentment.

I love Martha. She seems a gutsy woman, not afraid to speak her mind and obviously the boss of the family. She loves Jesus and loves using her gift of hospitality to bless Him and His friends. From Jesus' perspective, Martha, Mary and Lazarus are like family to Him. He loves to go to their home to chill out with His friends.

But on this particular day, after they turn up at Bethany, something seems different, for Martha is distracted. Jesus is telling stories, so Mary listens with the disciples and her brother.

Mary adores listening to Jesus. His words are enthralling and open doorways to things she's only ever imagined. She fixes her eyes on Him and, ignoring the clattering from the kitchen, drinks in His every word.

Martha would also have loved to listen to Jesus but felt too het up. She was very aware of all the expectations that rested on her as the eldest. Hospitality was her gift, but there was always so much pressure from other people. It's true that Jesus had invited everyone to sit with Him, but who else would provide the meal if she didn't?

So, while Mary feasted on Jesus' words, Martha stewed in silence, the only evidence of her growing resentment, the banging and crashing of her pots and pans.

Let's pause for a moment.

I keep getting the strong sense that for someone reading this, you too feel you've been dealt an unfair hand and others are taking advantage. Like Martha, you are struggling to focus on anything because you feel distracted and upset. You are pulled in all directions by the opinions of others, yet don't feel free to make your own path. I will come back to you, but let's look again at Martha.

It was when Martha peeped through the dividing curtain and noticed Mary's rapt expression as she gazed up at Jesus that she exploded. Pushing through the startled circle of listeners, she snapped at Jesus:

"Lord, don't you care that my sister has left me to do the work by myself? Tell her to help me!"

In the Throes of Resentment

Even as the words left her lips, she regretted them. How could she accuse her Lord of not caring? Yet deep down she *did* feel hurt. How could she have interrupted Him so rudely? She knew how important His teaching was, that was why she felt so upset to miss out. But she shouldn't have just barged in like that. How could He ever forgive her?

Coming back to you: the Lord says that, like Martha, you feel trapped because of other's expectations. You are in turmoil with feelings of anger, jealousy and hurt. You are hurting those close to you, but you feel stuck in the quicksand of resentment.

How did Jesus respond to Martha?

When Martha looked at Jesus she saw such love in His eyes as He gazed back at her. *"Martha, Martha..."* He said gently and her hard heart melted. Somehow, as He told her that He understood her upset, but that Mary had chosen rightly, she knew He loved her too. He understood, He cared and He forgave.

Reflect

If Jesus responded to Martha with such compassion, how is He responding to you?

God says:

"Beloved, beloved, you are mine. Sit in my embrace and drink in my love. Let me heal that wound of a lack of affirmation. I rejoice over you and love to be with you."

Extra Readings

Ephesians 4:1-6; 29-5:2

Day 7 – Prayer Empowered Love

(2 Kings 4:8-37)

"'Did I ask you for a son, my Lord?' she said. 'Didn't I tell you, don't raise my hopes?'"

This story moves me to tears because of the evidence of God's love running right through it. It is a glorious story, not just because of the miracle of the child coming back to life, but because love and prayer are so much at the forefront.

When God's love fills our hearts, we make a colossal impact for the kingdom of God just by being ourselves and allowing Him to love through us.

Do you realise that you carry the presence of God with you?

As I am writing I sense that for someone, you feel that you have nothing much to give. You see others doing great things for God, but you say, "All I can do is cook and serve people." I sensed God was laughing lovingly and saying, *"If only you could see the impact of the way you use your cooking and serving gifts, you would be dancing around in amazement."* Be encouraged and don't carry on comparing yourself with others, because the key is that you use your own gift with the fullness of God's love, just as you are doing.

This story opens with the well-to-do Shunammite woman inviting Elisha for a meal when he is near her home. This becomes a pattern of regular invitations. Then one day she goes further, saying to her husband,

"I know that this man ... is a holy man of God. Let's make a small room on the roof and put in it a bed and a table, a chair and a lamp for him. Then he can stay there whenever he comes to us."

The presence of God in Elisha has impacted her, moving her to serve him. She offers him a room as an act of worship. She doesn't have Elisha's faith; she can't prophesy or do miracles; but when her heart is touched and her hunger for a holy love is stirred, she does what she can and offers the extra space in her home.

Have you allowed your hunger for a holy love to be stirred?

How might God want you to give that love away?

I used to think that because of my deafness, my worship was inferior. But then I realised that God wanted me to be a worshipper, not a worship leader! He wanted me to offer what I had, not what I hadn't. He wanted my love.

How is God prompting *you* to worship?

This woman was touched by God and through her gift of a room, Elisha's heart was touched too. He wanted to give back to her and bless her for what she was giving him.

This is how our deserts can be transformed, as we recognise the gift of God's love in someone else, then find our hearts are also moved to love extravagantly.

When Elisha wanted to bless her, he heard that the woman was childless, so he listened to God. He then spoke God's decree over her that she would have a son.

Listening to God is powerful as it opens us up to receiving heavenly revelation.

Have you listened to God today?

Bad things still happen, even when God has been blessing us supernaturally. For this lady it is her worst nightmare when her miracle child suddenly dies. All thought vanishes except that she must go to Elisha.

Elisha's prayer-empowered love for her child is so moving. It is as if he is pouring his very own life into the boy, a picture of the future love of Jesus.

"He ... prayed to the Lord ... got on the bed and lay on the boy, mouth to mouth, eyes to eyes, hands to hands ... the boy's body grew warm."

Prayer

Thank you, Father, for the power of your love. Help me to pray and love from my whole heart. Amen.

Extra Readings

Mark 1:40-42; 1 Corinthians 13:1-8

45

Day 8 – The Lord will provide

(Genesis 22:1-18)

"Abraham looked up and there in a thicket he saw a ram caught by its horns. He went over and took the ram and sacrificed it as a burnt offering instead of his son."

Has the Lord ever asked you to give up something precious to you?

In today's story God asks Abraham to offer up his son, Isaac; the son Abraham and Sarah had waited so long for. They'd called him Isaac to remind them how they'd laughed at the idea of being parents in their old age. Was that laughter now about to turn to mourning?

God is love, but sometimes faith is hard to understand. Why did God tell Abraham to sacrifice the very son He'd miraculously given them? It makes me shiver that God would ask such a thing and that Abraham would obey. Who knows what questions were raging in Abraham's heart as he readied Isaac and himself for their trek into the wilderness?

Heaven is hidden to us and although God has called us into partnership with Him, we only see glimpses of what is to come and our picture of what He is doing is blurred.

"For we know in part and we prophesy in part, but when completeness comes, what is in part disappears." (1 Corinthians 13:9-10)

As we seek Him and grow in our ability to discern His voice, our insights become more accurate, but there is always the need to step out and trust because *"faith is the assurance of what we hope for and the certainty of what we do not see"* (Hebrews 11:1). Sometimes He just wants us to trust and obey.

God does not call us to *blindly* obey, but to trust out of our heart knowledge of Him and His character. Abraham had been building this knowledge in his heart as he experienced God's guidance and faithfulness through years of knowing Him. He didn't understand why, but He did know God. So, when Isaac queried where the lamb was for the sacrifice, Abraham's answer came from a heart that was at rest in God:

"God Himself will provide the lamb for the burnt offering, my son."

When I first became a Christian, I had to give up horse riding as the only time the stables could have me was a Sunday morning. As a child I'd always dreamt of having my own pony, but it just wasn't possible. Taking riding lessons after I started college seemed a great alternative. I loved horses and having struggled throughout my childhood, there was something about climbing onto the back of an animal so much bigger than me, yet safe and loving, that I found very powerful. Also, there was the fact that despite its size I was in charge! I believe now that it was God who led me to start riding lessons and maybe the horses helped me take my first steps out of my fears.

Nevertheless, I knew I would have to give up the horses. It was hard because I was finding church a struggle with my deafness, but it was so worth it and I know that if I hadn't made that choice my life may have been very different

Reflect

Are you willing to obey God in something He has put on your heart, even if it seems impossible?

Are you afraid of what He might ask of you?

God says:

"Don't be afraid, for I am wholly good and trustworthy in all my ways. I will never ask you to do anything that is wrong for you, but I will ask you to do things that will stretch you and cause you to put your faith in me. Your faith is the most precious gift you have ever received. Guard it carefully and use it with great joy and you will be amazed at what I will do for and through you."

Extra Readings

1 Kings 17:7-16; Hebrews 12:1-3

Day 9 – Welcoming Today

(Hebrews 3:7-8)

"As the Holy Spirit says, 'Today if you hear His voice, do not harden your hearts.'"

As I started today's reading, I sensed that someone is in a wilderness of greyness. You feel dispirited and flat, as if all colour and adventure has drained away. Today is just another hard day to get through as best you can, and you can't imagine that ever changing. But the Lord is there with you in the midst of your weariness and is calling you to open your heart to the hope that He can transform your today as you walk in partnership with Him.

By nature, I am a procrastinator and am always running away from today. If I can put something off to another day, I will. But the other day I realised that I was waking up each morning with a feeling of dread about the day's tasks and aware that so many jobs were accumulating because of having put them off. Suddenly the Lord spoke into my heart, showing me that I was losing my sense of the wonder of each day being a gift from Him – an opportunity to enjoy His presence in a unique way, and also to know His enabling.

I was going through each day in a *"I've got to get this done"* mode, but He wanted me to treasure the day, listen for His voice and recognise that each day He gives special things to discover more of His love and grace. The book of Hebrews quotes from Deuteronomy, where God tells the Israelites, *"Today, if you hear His voice, do not harden your hearts."* They hardened their hearts out of rebellion, but that hardening can come about just as much through having a negative, defeatist lack of joy, even if we are not rebelling against Him. As I thought about this and my attitude to *today* I wrote the following poem, which I found helpful myself and maybe you will too.

Hello Today

Today has dawned
It's already several hours in
And I am an important part of it.

My shadow will fall on the ground and the walls today.
And where I am, no one else can stand in that moment of time.
I often start each day full of inertia,
One day just like any other.
But today I want to befriend Today,
To discover what you look like
To see with your eyes and hear with your ears.

What does it feel like to be a day that slips by unnoticed?
When the reason for your existence is to be loved and enjoyed?
My destiny is that Today is part of my life.
I am destined to influence Today, and Today will influence me.

So, hello Today, it's lovely to see you.
I am sorry for the times I've allowed my struggles to blind me
to your beauty.
I want to explore you today,
To see what wonders you have in store for me.
And even when things are hard, to see what secret strengths
Of joy and faith you want me to discover in myself.

So, hello Today and welcome to my life.
I will never see you again after this day ends
So, let's enjoy it together to the full.

Reflect

God is with you today and wants to bless you. As the Psalmist
said, *"This is the day that the Lord has made. Let us rejoice and
be glad in it"* (Psalm 118:24).

Spend some time thanking the Lord for the gift of today and
ask Him how He wants to bless you in it. Listen for His voice.
Is there any particular blessing He wants to give you today?
Thank Him for it and start to look out for it as you go through
the day.

Extra Reading

Genesis 1:1-2:3

Day 10 – A Healing Encounter

(John 4:7-30)

"The woman said, 'I know that Messiah, [called Christ] is coming. When he comes He will explain everything to us.' Then Jesus declared, 'I who speak to you, am He.'"

This story is enthralling, bringing alive the fact that God always loves to engage with us. Whatever we are doing, whether we are on a spiritual high or our life is in a mess, God still chooses to be with us and never gives up loving us. This story conveys the wonder of God's mercy in choosing us to be His friends, despite our weaknesses and failures. He loves to draw us into intimacy and to give us divine revelation that will both heal and empower us.

Maybe, like the Samaritan woman, you've made wrong choices and as a result are suffering shame or isolation? It is telling that this woman came to draw her water at noon. It was unheard of to do so, because of the intensity of the sun's heat. But it was imperative that she avoided other people because of the shame she constantly carried – which others wouldn't hesitate to rebuke her for. She was lonely and had lost all hope of ever making a new start in life.

Some of us find we are in a wilderness through no fault of our own; through painful circumstances like bereavement or rejection. But the wilderness of shame and regret is a harsh one indeed. If you are in that position today, take a few minutes to reflect personally on this story, offering Him all your regrets. What does God want to say to you?

I love the way that Jesus responds to God's prompting and lovingly reaches out to her. He is not put off by her hard demeanour but opens up a conversation. He knows, through the Holy Spirit, about her deepest sins, but the first thing He says is, "Will you give me a drink?" How incredible that He spoke not about her mistakes, but into the area of her anointing to serve that had long since shut down. He then revealed His knowledge of her life, but so lovingly that she was amazed rather than crushed. He always speaks to heal and transform, never to destroy us.

When I was first a Christian and struggling because of years of abuse, some Christian friends asked if I could stay and look after their children when the wife had her new baby. I couldn't believe they'd asked *me*, for I was not only full of shame but also very impractical. Accepting they'd chosen me was a big step forward in my own healing.

Amazingly, the Samaritan woman was the first person that Jesus told He was the expected Messiah. How awesome that He trusted her, a broken woman, to receive such incredible revelation. But Jesus has no favourites and wants to encourage you to expect Him to speak to you in amazing ways too.

Right now, He is with you and wants to bathe you with His transforming love. His words will empower you to step out of your inner wilderness of shame into a new place of joyful partnership with Him.

Knowing that He accepts us completely and wants to give us divine revelation, releases us to fulfil our God-given destinies. Like the Samaritan woman, we too will experience transformation as we listen for His voice.

Prayer

Lord Jesus, thank you for your mercy and love. Thank you that you've chosen me despite my many sins. Thank you for the wonder of knowing that you desire to give me new levels of revelation and insight. Your words are so powerful and freeing. Please help me, Lord, just as you did that woman, to live as the person you made me to be. Amen.

Extra Readings

Psalm 57; 2 Corinthians 5:16-21

Day 11 – God-given Strength to Choose Well

(Ruth 1:1-18)

"'Look,' said Naomi, 'your sister-in-law is going back to her people and her gods. Go back with her.' But Ruth replied, 'Don't urge me to leave you or to turn back from you. Where you go, I will go....'"

The amazing thing about Ruth was her ability to choose well in the midst of great personal loss. In a short space of time she had lost both her husband and her father-in-law. Now Naomi is moving away and her sister-in-law is going back to her family. In that kind of situation many people, including myself, would struggle to make decisions. We flail around in the wilderness of uncertainty, our minds paralysed with all the choices.

I feel for someone reading this that you are in that position right now and feel very alone and helpless. God wants to bring you His comfort and strength and to reassure you that even though you feel weak, He has given you *"a spirit of power, and of love and of a calm and well-balanced mind"* (2 Timothy 1:7 AMP). With His enabling, you will be able to make wise choices. Recovering from loss is a journey and the pain can't be transformed overnight as it takes time to work through the grief. But God is alongside us and His gift of calm and soundness of mind is very precious.

Ruth's story encourages us deeply. I often feel that I don't make good choices and allow others to make my decisions for me. I am a people pleaser and fearful of choosing things that may imply I'm always putting myself first. Ruth shows us what it means to willingly give up everything you love in order to help another, without being a doormat. She was a woman who was filled with love, knew what she wanted to do and did it with certainty and peace.

There is always someone who will advise us. Their counsel may be very wise and it's important to listen because God may guide us through them. However, seeking counsel can become a means of abdicating responsibility for our own choices. Are we fearful of trusting in our own ability to hear God and to be in tune with our own hearts?

Naomi advised both Ruth and Orpah to return to their own people, so they could remarry and have children. Orpah followed this counsel, but Ruth heard a different voice, the voice of sacrificial love. This voice said it was more important to stay close to the one she'd come to love as her own mother. Ruth was neither arrogant nor cowed. She obviously respected Naomi with all her heart and yet she respected herself too. She believed in herself enough to know that her own heart was directing her in the right course of action and that was the voice she needed to follow. This ultimately brought Ruth the wonderful reward of marrying Boaz and becoming part of Jesus' genealogy. Awesome!

Let's listen humbly to others and then bring their counsel into the throne room of our own hearts. God will whisper to us there and guide us with His peace.

God says:

"Beloved one, you have been mocked in your opinions and I see how you now let them fall to the ground rather than be mocked again. But I have given you the mind of Christ and your heart is my home. Do not be afraid, beloved one. Dare to see and love yourself as I see and love you. Dare to listen to your heart and you will know the reward of my peace and blessing."

Extra readings

1 Corinthians 2:9-16; Proverbs 2:13-24

Day 12 – Joy

(Isaiah 35)

"Water will gush forth in the wilderness and streams in the desert."

Today we are encouraged by Isaiah's beautiful prophecy of redemption and joy. God is declaring what He is bringing about and the picture He paints is one of transformation, worship, beauty, peace and community. No wilderness can remain in its natural state when God is bringing this new life to birth. While we may view our personal wildernesses very negatively, God sees them differently. They are a springboard for Him to bring about His glorious redemptive plans, where everything that is parched, dry, dying, empty, or pain-filled is wonderfully refreshed and transformed.

Whatever wilderness you face, God has a redemptive plan for you. Even Creation itself has been designed to reflect and express the joy of God's presence and beauty. I was talking with a friend and she shared how even in the depths of the oceans where no one can see, the extravagance of detail and colour woven into every living thing is mind blowing. Earth is a tiny glimpse of the un-decaying beauty of heaven and God left clues to His glory, character and ways in all He made so that we might know Him. As Paul teaches us in Romans 1:20,

"For since the creation of the world, God's invisible qualities, his eternal power and divine nature have been clearly seen, being understood from what has been made."

At this present time, it is spring. The trees are blossoming and tulips and daffodils are bursting into bloom. God has been speaking to me through this glorious season of new growth and beauty, showing me afresh that He is the God who makes all things new:

"Forget the former things, do not dwell on the past. See, I am doing a new thing. Now it springs up, do you not perceive it? I am making a way in the wilderness and streams in the wasteland." (Isaiah 43:18-19)

This passage and especially the words *"forget the former things,"* spoke to me very profoundly about 5 years after I became a Christian. Deep down I was still feeling a victim. I personalised every negative remark, even when they were not aimed at me. I knew God loved me, but could never connect with that emotionally because of my constant self-rejection. But God was saying, *"You are so beautiful to me, the very apple of my eye. Now is the time to let those old lies go and to stop agreeing with them."*

My life felt desolate and I couldn't see any beauty, but He could. As I chose to believe and accept His words of love, my wilderness changed and became beautiful with hope, joy, love and deep peace.

At another level, Isaiah's prophecy is looking ahead to heaven and all the joy and wonder that awaits us there. God has given us amazing prophetic pictures of what is to come, so that we can be strengthened and envisioned as we pass through the difficulties of life and indeed as we approach death.

Marilyn and I had a blind friend in her early 50's who was dying of cancer. She'd been praying for healing, believing there were things God still wanted her to do, but despite many people praying, she was not healed. This was a real wilderness for our friend and although she did come to accept it, there was still great sadness. We were with her on the night she died and she was mostly in an induced sleep, but every few minutes she would half sit in a very alert way and say, "Wow!" When she passed into eternity she was totally at peace with a "Wow" on her lips!

Reflect

Read this whole chapter slowly and prayerfully and ask the Lord to pinpoint any areas in your life that need His renewal and beauty. Thank Him that He already has a place in heaven for you.

Extra Reading

Isaiah 61:1-4

Day 13 – In the Agony of Loss

(Luke 7:11-17)

"Deep in earth my love is lying. And I must weep alone."[2]

"When the Lord saw her, His heart went out to her and He said, 'Don't cry.'"

Are you missing someone dear to you? Losing someone we love is one of the most crippling things we can ever endure and even when a relationship has been difficult, the loss of that person can still cause great emotional pain.

My stepfather died some years ago. He had abused me as a child, but I got through those years by burying all my emotions. When he died it was as if the lid came off and I was filled with sorrow. The grief journey is different for us all, but many feel as if all the joy and beauty in life has been sucked away. As if they are in an arid, grey land where tears are their only constant.

Are you in that place, watching the world go by as if you are no longer part of it? Do you feel lonely even in the midst of a

---

[2] Edgar Allan Poe

crowd? Is your heart aching as you struggle to cope because all you can do is cry?

God cares and is with you. Try to take a moment to read this story in Luke 7. The widow of Nain knew about grief. Her husband had already died and together with her only son she'd been struggling to survive. Now her son had also died. As she stumbled behind his coffin, the pain in her heart was all consuming. What hope was there for her now? She was without support in the world.

The Bible says that when Jesus saw her, *"His heart went out to her."* Jesus never sympathises from a distance. He feels our pain as if it is His own. When He says *"Don't cry"* it is because He Himself carries our tears and weeps with us. He wants us to know that He loves us, understands our pain and cares deeply. But this story also shows that He acts to restore our joy and gives us new hope in the most incredible ways.

Marilyn and I once prayed for a very distressed lady who was recently widowed. Unable to hear her, I prayed quietly. Suddenly a picture came to my mind of someone standing before a beautiful house. The door opened and I saw a majestic figure in the doorway surrounded by light. He welcomed the person to enter in. I caught a brief glimpse of the beautiful interior and then they were inside and the door closed. There was a real sense of joy and I knew the Lord was saying He had welcomed her husband home. The lady was amazed. Unbeknown to me, she had shared with Marilyn her fear that her husband was not saved when he died. This fear was tormenting and preventing her from receiving God's peace, but Jesus saw her anguish and longed to touch her with true comfort, just as He longs to touch you today.

Reflect

Take a moment quietly. Jesus is with you in your pain. Think of those words, *"His heart went out to her."* What does it mean to you that His heart goes out to you? Imagine Him sitting and reaching out to comfort you. What will you say to Him? How does He bring you new hope?

Prayer

Lord Jesus, thank you that you are alongside me and your heart goes out to me. In my anguish hold me in the comfort of your love. Speak into my despair with your words of life. Touch me with the miracle of your resurrection power. Amen.

Extra Readings

John 11:11-35; Psalm 56:8; Isaiah 61:1-5

Day 14 – Pruning

(John 15:1-17)

"I am the true vine and my Father is the gardener. He cuts off every branch in me that bears no fruit, while every branch that does bear fruit he prunes so that it will be even more fruitful."

Today I have a distinct sense that someone is struggling with depression and feelings of inferiority because your life feels so unfruitful compared to others.

What we believe about ourselves has great power and, sadly, if we believe very negative things they can become self-fulfilling prophecies. In Matthew 25:14–30 the servant who is given just one talent buries it rather than putting it to use because he fears his master, who is actually a good man.

What good is money if it's buried in the ground?

What good will our lives be if we bury the gifts God has given us?

We need to see that God has not destined us to live in competition/comparison with each other, but in unique fruitfulness.

He is the gardener and is working to bring out the best in *every* plant in His garden.

In this passage in John 15, I often skip these words about the Father cutting off the unfruitful branches and pruning others back. It's quite a scary thought, especially when you struggle with low self-esteem. What constitutes being fruitful in God's eyes? Will I fail and be cut off from Him? What kind of things will need pruning back?

Remember that this passage is written from the perspective of God's love for us. He loves us as He loves His Son, Jesus. He created us with the seeds of fruitfulness woven into our identity, so He is not asking us to strive to be something unattainable, but to simply be who we already are in Him.

Last Spring a friend discovered that our lovely camellia plant had lots of dead foliage hanging over the top, which was draining the life from the rest of the plant and killing off the flowers. If we'd left it, the whole camellia would have died, so we cut all the dead growth out. The camellia was saved, although it was too late to get many flowers then. This Spring, however, we are seeing the fruit of that drastic surgery as it is now resplendent in blooms and more beautiful than ever before.

One damaged branch had a catastrophic effect, but cutting it out had an even greater effect for the good. What branches in our lives may God need to cut out so that we may all the more reveal the presence of Jesus?

The things that deaden us include the lies we believe about ourselves. For example, that we don't deserve His love or that everyone despises us. Other "dead" branches can spring from our refusal to forgive or allowing bitterness to grow in our hearts. Just as the dead foliage overshadowed the healthy part of our plant, negative beliefs can overshadow everything else in our lives and the only remedy is to allow God to cut them out. In other words, we have to yield them to Him and choose not to hang onto them anymore.

Just as our camellia is now beautiful again, so our lives will be full of the colour and fragrance of His beauty when we truly allow Him to be the Gardener.

Reflect

Spend some time outside.

If you notice anything that's overgrown or has dead foliage, ask the Lord if there's anything in your life that it represents.

Lift any insights up to Him, spending time asking what He wants you to do. Remember He loves you 100%

Prayer

Thank you, Father, that you love me and have joyfully created me to be a unique expression of your loveliness. I give you permission to prune or cut out anything in me that is dead or stifling your beauty within me. Thank you that I can trust you and your amazing love for me. Amen.

Extra Reading

Acts 9:1-19

Day 15 – The Barren Place of Rebellion

(Deuteronomy 1:26-45)

"But you were unwilling to go up; you rebelled against the command of the Lord your God. You grumbled in your tents and said, 'The Lord hates us.'"

One of the saddest biblical stories is that of the Israelites wandering in the desert for forty years because of their rebellion. They had seen God do amazing miracles: sending plagues against the Egyptians; opening up the Red Sea; guiding them by fire and cloud; bringing water out of rocks...

But despite this, their hearts were not captivated by God's glory. In their minds, Moses was the one who knew God and they were the ones who followed.

I find myself wondering, how well do I do in this regard?

When I attend a service where God is doing amazing things, or read an inspiring testimony, do I allow my heart to be captivated by God? Or do I remain enslaved by the walls I put up as a child? Some of us grew up in survival mode and those inner walls were essential, but if we don't yield them to God we become enslaved and fear becomes our master. Yet, Jesus frees us from that prison, as Paul teaches:

"The spirit you received does not make you slaves so that you live in fear again; rather the Spirit you received brought about your adoption to sonship. And by Him we cry 'Abba, Father.'" (Romans 8:15)

The Israelites had been oppressed by the Egyptians for 400 years, but now they were in a new place and it was vital they listened to God, who had promised to lead them into this new land. Instead they listened to the negatives:

"We can't attack these people, they are stronger than we are ... The land devours those living in it, all the people we saw there are of great size ... We seemed like grasshoppers in our own eyes and we looked the same to them." (Numbers 13:31–33)

Fear magnifies things and it only takes one fear-filled report to infect a whole group of people:

"That night all the members of the community raised their voices and wept aloud. All the Israelites grumbled against Moses and Aaron..." (Numbers 14:1)

We see this today in the way the media puts out fear-infused reports. It's easy to get sucked in without realising their deadly effects. The Israelites believed that the Anakites saw them as powerless, although the opposite was probably true.

The truth is, when we listen to fear, we become what we listen to.

Another reason why the Israelites were wandering in the desert for forty years was their grumbling. Moses said that, *"[they] grumbled in their tents."*

Why would something as basic as grumbling have had such a drastic effect?

I looked grumbling up and some of its synonyms were quite telling: complain, moan, whine, mutter, protest, criticise, accuse…

Don't these words remind you of coffee time after the Sunday service?!

I'm being facetious, but there is some truth in it. We love to pick holes in things rather than encourage, build up and glorify God. The sad thing about the Israelites was how they thought and talked about God.

"[They] grumbled … and said 'the Lord hates us…'"

Because they listened to fear rather than the Lord, first their thoughts and then their words were corrupted. They turned away from God's true character, defamed Him and ended up in the wilderness.

Reflect

If I say to you, "God loves you," does your heart say "YES" or deep down do you dismiss it?

If God asks you to step out of your comfort zone and do something different, is your reaction one of excitement and confidence in God's help, or are you fearful?

Talk to Him about the insights that came to you just now, as you answered these questions, and ask Him to free you from any fear holding you back.

Prayer

Father, I am so sorry for the way I've allowed myself to be sucked into the culture of fear, grumbling and negativity. Lord, I long to know and be confident in your love from the depths of my being. I give to you all my inner walls that have enslaved me and ask you to fill me with new boldness and joy in following you. Amen.

Extra Readings

Jeremiah 1:4-8; Romans 12:1-2

Day 16 – The Lord is my Shepherd

(Psalm 23:1-3)

"The Lord is my shepherd; I lack nothing. He makes me lie down in green pastures; He leads me beside quiet waters; He restores my soul."

Where are you on your journey through the wilderness today? Sometimes journeys can be full of the wonder of seeing new things and having new experiences. At other times they become wearisome and we may worry we haven't got all the resources we need.

David begins his heartfelt description of the Lord as his shepherd by focusing on the Lord's care for him. *"I will not lack"* he says. This is a great example of Spirit-inspired positive self-talk. He was telling his innermost being, "You won't lack, God Himself is looking after you. He is your shepherd. He knows exactly what help you need..."

Like many of us, David knew rejection and his circumstances were far from comfortable. He was out in the wilds day and night, with the sheep his only companions. Facing danger on every side from gangs and wild animals, the inhospitable terrain made his job as a shepherd very difficult.

Are you, like David, feeling lonely and daunted at the moment? How are you dealing with it? The Lord is your shepherd just as much as He was David's. He is there to guide you to those still waters where you can drink and be at rest.

David also affirmed that, *"He guides me along the right paths for His name's sake."* Many paths in the desert are dangerous, even deadly. Similarly, some of the paths we take when we respond to difficulties can be deadly. A friend recently experienced bullying at work. She didn't know what to do or who she could talk to, so squashed all her feelings down in an effort to cope, but that has resulted in deep depression and anger.

What kind of path have you chosen? Is it working for you?

David's way was to walk the path of healing. He opened his heart up to the Lord and discovered the wonder of His provision and care. He then began reminding himself of how lovingly God was looking after him and would continue to guide and provide for him.

How did David come to know the Lord as his shepherd? I believe David began to sense the Lord speaking to him through the things he was doing every day. In other words, his very job became a channel of God's voice to him.

Do we expect God to speak to us like this, even to use our jobs as a channel for His voice?

The Lord is *my* shepherd, David wrote, hearing God's whisper as he gently called the sheep by name and led them to a new grazing area.

Will God reassure you and me like that? Remember He has no favourites.

One day I was in a bad mood because of an argument. Suddenly, as I carefully ironed a blouse, I realised I was ensuring the blouse looked its best by using the right heat for the delicate material. Suddenly, these thoughts dropped into my mind:

"You iron your blouse with great care because you know exactly how you want it to look. You have that picture in your mind's eye and you work on it accordingly. In the same way I see you as beautiful and know exactly how to bring that beauty about. You see only the creases, but when I look at you I see the beauty of my precious son."

I was stunned and realised how deeply God loved me as He drew me onto a path of affirmation and peace instead of anger and regret.

Reflect

As your shepherd, God wants to guide you into a place of soul restoration. He is alongside you and encourages you to listen for His whisper today.

Prayer

Thank you, Lord, that you are my shepherd and with you I lack nothing. Amen.

Extra Readings

John 10:27-30; Philippians 4:18-19

Day 17 – When We Cry Out to the Lord

(1 Samuel 1:17-18)

"Eli answered, 'Go in peace and may the God of Israel grant you what you have asked of Him.' She said 'May your servant find favour in your eyes.' Then she went her way and ate something and her face was no longer downcast."

Are you feeling downcast today? As I was praying I sensed that someone is despairing. You are downcast, which literally means, downward looking. You have lost hope and have no energy left to even try to look up and seek God's love or to pray anymore.

In this story we see how Hannah was also stuck in a desert of hopelessness. Her heart was breaking because of her inability to have children, plus the constant cruelty of her rival, Penninah. Penninah's mockery went on year after year. We can find it crushing when we hear one negative word, but for Hannah it carried on until she couldn't eat, couldn't enjoy her husband's love and couldn't participate in the joy of the Jewish festivals. She was in a deep depression.

If you are struggling under a similar weight of hopelessness today, God feels your pain and longs to comfort and hold you close to His heart. Hannah needed that comfort too. She felt alone and even her husband didn't seem to understand. He wanted his love to be enough, but sometimes our brokenness goes deeper, and even what our loved ones can give us doesn't seem enough.

Hannah was at the end of herself, but God was there and it was actually when she realised she couldn't go on that the seeds were sown for change. Verses 9–11 describe how Hannah suddenly stood up at the feast and, moving away from everyone else, began to pray.

She had been imprisoned by her endless heartbreak, too embittered to even think about making changes. But at this feast she suddenly snapped and started to cry out to the Lord. Maybe she'd never shared her feelings with Him before or maybe there was just one mocking word too many? For whatever reason, something within Hannah shifted. From being a crushed victim she got up and began to pray.

Initially, it didn't appear to make any difference, for as well as Penninah's mockery, the high priest now accused her of being drunk! How could Eli be so blind to the truth? Sometimes, sadly, even our spiritual leaders make terrible judgements and add to our pain.

If you have been similarly judged, God wants you to know that He never judges you. Unlike Eli, He always sees right into your heart. He hears every cry and He stores every tear. He understands and cares so much for you.

We all experience being judged unfairly at times. The key to our transformation is, how will we react?

Hannah could have become even more crushed or angry.

But she didn't.

With dignity she told Eli the truth, that she was simply praying. It is clear that God was already at work for Eli now changed in his attitude and started declaring God's blessing over her.

We read that when Hannah left him *"she ate something and her face was no longer downcast."*

God answered her prayer and ultimately gave her Samuel. But more significantly, with God's empowering, Hannah started to take steps out of the desert of hopelessness into the garden of hope. She looked up instead of down; she ate; she chose life.

Reflect

Think about your life. Are you like Hannah, feeling crushed by your circumstances or the actions of those close to you? How have you reacted? Spend some time with the Lord, knowing He is with you and cares so much for you. If you can, cry out to Him with your longings and tears.

Extra readings

2 Corinthians 1:2-4; Mark 5:25-34

Day 18 – You are the Potter, I am the Clay

(Jeremiah 18:1-6)

"I went down to the potter's house and I saw him working at the wheel. But the pot he was shaping from the clay was marred in his hands, so the potter formed it into another pot shaping it as seemed best to him. Then the word of the Lord came to me, 'Can I not do with you as this potter does?' declares the Lord."

Something that always pushes me into a desert of negativity is when I feel I don't match up to others. It can be the most mundane things that make me feel a failure. For example, I was cooking roast lamb for a friend, but the meat came out very tough. I thought it was my fault and vowed never to cook lamb again! I lost confidence in my ability to be hospitable. In reality, it may have needed better cooking, but it could just as easily have been a poor joint. Like many of us, I chose to see failure on very weak evidence.

God sees things differently and wants us to focus on His persevering love and trust in us. As I was reading this passage I sensed Him speaking to me through the story of the potter reworking the marred clay into something new and beautiful.

He is undeterred by the weaknesses that appear in the clay, even if they seem to destroy his original plan for it.

I found myself becoming aware of all the things that make me feel marred: hurts from the past; areas of fear and anger; wounds caused by lies of rejection and abuse. I identified with that lump of clay and the fear of being discarded and replaced by a better piece. As I meditated, God drew close and showed me how often I reject myself, believing that I am lacking; that any gifts I have will be passed over by Him in favour of someone more capable.

Are you struggling with such feelings too, and holding back from being the person you know God is calling you to be?

What do you think God wants to say to you?

God desires for us to believe we are loved and chosen by Him. The potter had a picture in his mind of the beautiful object that the marred clay could still become. I believe God is saying to us all today:

"Will you allow yourself to rest in my hands and know that I love you? Will you accept that I have always known about the things that have weakened and even marred you, but they have never altered my love or my plans for you? Will you allow yourself to soften in the deepest and hardest areas of your being? To feel the gentleness of my touch moulding you with love, weeping over and washing away the knotty lumps of pain, working in gentleness and care so deep within you?

Will you believe that I am the one who never gives up on you, but perseveres to make you something so beautiful, whole, unique and delighted in? Trust in me and let me love you into wholeness and beauty. In my hands, your weaknesses becomes chinks that my radiant light can shine through to others. Rest in the hollow of my hand and know that you are held there forever. Let my fingers gently do their work of bringing life anew into the deepest parts."

Prayer

Thank you, dear Lord. You are my maker. You are the potter, I am the clay. Your works are wonderful. Help me to know that and to be at rest in all you are doing in my life. Amen.

Extra Readings

Jeremiah 1:6-8; 2 Corinthians 3:18

Day 19 – When Everything Goes Wrong

(Luke 24:13-35)

"As they talked and discussed these things with each other, Jesus came and walked along with them, but they were kept from recognising Him."

Sometimes, all we can think of is escaping. Putting distance between ourselves and an intolerable situation seems the only way to find relief from the pain.

If you are going through such a time, God cares and is with you. I feel that you are so weighed down that you cannot even cry. You are locked in a dark place and your heart feels like a stone.

Cleopas and his friend knew those unbearable feelings and were running from them. Scripture says that as they made their way to Emmaus they talked together, but when the One they were mourning walked alongside them they didn't recognise Him.

What kept them from seeing Him?

Are there times when you too fail to recognise Jesus?

These disciples had travelled with Him, heard Him preaching and witnessed His amazing miracles, but as He talked with them now, they didn't know His voice.

Are you in a similar place?

When Jesus questioned them, we read that their faces were downcast. That literally means they were throwing their attention onto the ground. They were looking down, not up. How then could they recognise Jesus?

What about the way they were talking? It's obvious their words were full of negativity. Even when they share about the women, far from their account being a source of wonder and faith, it's the last straw to these disciples. They preface this statement with the words, *"and what is more..."* as if it was just another terrible thing.

But that is the nature of the desert of deep disappointment.

It makes us look down.

It makes us speak negatively.

It stops us from recognising Jesus.

It makes us slow to believe.

These disciples had been given an incredible opportunity to enjoy the company of the newly resurrected Jesus. He wanted them to know an overflow of joy and healing from the trauma they'd experienced

He wanted quality time with His friends.

But although, with hindsight, they later realised that their "hearts were burning while He opened the Scriptures" they failed to connect that inner witness with the truth of who this stranger was.

Knowing all of this, Jesus still loved them and wanted them to understand the good news. He chose to walk alongside them. He asked them questions and responded by opening up God's word to them. He so touched them that they insisted He stay with them when they reached their destination. I love what followed, for it was when Jesus blessed the bread at the start of the meal and began to pass it to them, that they suddenly realised: *this is Jesus!*

It was the familiar gesture of a dearly loved friend that opened the door to their understanding. In that moment of seeing Him do what He'd done countless times before, the dots joined up and suddenly they could see. The desert was transformed, their lethargy replaced with a passion to return home and share their good news.

Jesus came to them through a familiar gesture.

How might that happen for you and me?

Once when I was on a silent retreat, there was soup served in shallow bowls. I am unsteady and wasn't sure how to carry the soup without spilling it. Suddenly, a lady turned round and with a twinkle in her eye mimed that she would take it for me. I'd been struggling emotionally, but Jesus touched me deeply through her simple gesture. Since then I've recognised Him on many occasions reaching out to me through someone's act of kindness. It never fails to open my eyes to the joy and hope of Jesus within me.

Reflect

What does it mean to you that Jesus came and walked alongside the disciples that day?

Have there been times when you've run away (either literally or emotionally) from a painful situation? Ask God to show you what He was doing for you at that time.

The disciple's hearts were "burning" as Jesus spoke with them. Ask Him what He wants to tell you that will open your heart to His love.

Thank Him that He always walks closely alongside you.

Extra Reading

Matthew 13:11-17

Day 20 – A Time of Testing

(Matthew 3:16-4:11)

"Then Jesus was led by the Spirit into the desert to be tempted by the devil. After fasting for forty days and forty nights he was hungry. The tempter came to him and said, 'If you are the Son of God tell these stones to become bread.'"

Are deserts always bad places to be?

Many wilderness situations come about because of deep struggles in our lives like bereavement, disappointment, illness... It's comforting to know that God transforms such situations with His love. But what about those times when God draws us into the wilderness Himself?

In this fascinating story we see how Jesus was led by the Spirit into the wilderness, to fast for forty days and endure temptation.

I wonder how it felt for Jesus, to have had such an amazing encounter with God when He was baptised, only to immediately be banished by the Spirit into the wilderness? His Father had publicly declared how pleased He was with Him and that He was beloved, so what was happening now?

Sometimes it can be hard to understand what God is doing, but it is vital that we grow in our faith to ensure we can fight the attacks of the evil one. If Satan was attacking Jesus' identity, he will certainly attack us in the same way. As with Jesus, this will often happen at just the point when we've had some kind of spiritual breakthrough. Satan hates us to hear the truth and for us to be strong in our relationship with God, so will use every means he can to whisper lies into our hearts. Strength does not just happen automatically, but grows as we use our spiritual muscles. Jesus needed to stand strong in the truth. Every time Satan came at Him with a lie or a temptation, Jesus refuted it with the words *"It is written..."* The power of God's word prevailed and Satan left Him.

Have you had to take your stand against the enemy's lies?

Are you secure in the foundation of God's love for you?

Could the Spirit be drawing you into a barren place in order for you to grow deeper in your inner strength and godliness?

What might that look like today, as not many of us can literally fast for over a month in a desert!

For some of us it may be through our circumstances not being what we'd hoped for.

A friend recently moved nearer her family, but that involved leaving her church family and friends. It proved a very hard move as, apart from her family, she knew no one else and couldn't find a church she felt comfortable in. Also, while taking from her, her family gave nothing back. She felt abandoned and confused. Was the enemy attacking her or had she been mistaken in believing the Lord had told her to go?

It's when these questions fill our hearts and our circumstances seem very different to what we'd hoped for that we have a choice. Will we just sink into disappointment and become cynical or will we trust that God is at work, and in His love is doing something far greater than we could ever imagine? Jesus came through that wilderness experience full of the power of the Holy Spirit, speaking with authority and ministering healing and deliverance. His time of testing released Him into His destiny as the Messiah.

As you open your heart to God and take your stand against the lies of the enemy, what will God start releasing you into?

Prayer

Lord Jesus, thank you that you went through the wilderness for me. Forgive me for my cynical reactions to difficulties. I choose to believe that you love me with an everlasting love and have chosen me for a purpose. Help me to stand on the foundation of your Word against every lie of the evil one. Amen.

Extra Readings

1 Peter 1:3-9; James 4:7-10

Day 21 – He Called my Name

A short story based on the account of Zacchaeus

(Luke 19:1-10)

"Zacchaeus, come down immediately, I must stay at your house today."

Panting for breath, Zacchaeus shoved through the crowd. He longed to see Jesus and the moment was within his grasp. Jesus had entered Jericho's gates and was coming along the road. People had been gathering all day to see Him. The excitement was intense, the rumours rife. No one talked directly to Zacchaeus – why would they?

Earlier that day Zacchaeus had sat in his tax collector's booth and strained his ears to eavesdrop conversations, hearing sensational claims. "Miracles like no other," one man said. "That blind man's eyes just started seeing," a tough looking merchant responded. "The food multiplied in their hands," exclaimed a woman, her eyes shining under her veil.

Zacchaeus was so caught up that he almost forgot people hated him.

"So who do you think He is?" he asked one man, who had been excitedly describing to a friend how a leper's skin had been made smooth again. Zacchaeus was mortified when the man slammed his coins down and, face averted, disappeared into the crowd.

"You traitor," hissed someone else, spitting in Zacchaeus' direction. "You don't think Jesus will be interested in you, do you? He'll know what you've done."

Zacchaeus was serving the Romans. Power was on his side, but as he cursed and decided to raise the taxes once again, he had never felt more lonely. "If only..." he began to think, but no, he had made his choice. He couldn't go back.

Jesus would soon be passing and Zacchaeus really wanted to see Him. Cursing his shortness, he pushed through the massed bodies, not caring who he shoved out of the way. Something was pulling him to Jesus. He didn't understand it, because he knew that if the people were right – if Jesus really did know everything – then He wouldn't even look at Zacchaeus. So why this longing to be near Him?

The crowd pressed harder and more people pushed into the narrow road. Excitement was pulsing. Whispers turned into shouts. How was he ever going to see Jesus? It was pointless.

Then he saw the huge sycamore tree rising in his path. It had densely covered branches about halfway up. That was it! He would climb the tree. Up there he would be able to see Jesus, but wouldn't have to face the shame of His rejection.

Energised, Zacchaeus scaled the tree and pushed through the dense foliage. In a few minutes he found the perfect branch. He expected shouts of derision from the crowd to follow him, but no one seemed to notice. Hidden by the thick leaves, he was just in time. A throng was pushing along the road, crowds shoving to get near the man in the middle. A cry, a chant: "Jesus, son of David, Lord…"

Jesus drew closer. Zacchaeus peered down, safe in the knowledge that Jesus couldn't see him. He looked ordinary. Yet there was something completely magnetic about Him.

If only he could speak to Jesus. But no, a great sadness filled Zacchaeus' heart for he knew that Jesus would have no choice but to reject him. He was pure and holy and Zacchaeus was scum.

"Forgive me, Lord," Zacchaeus whispered, peering down, "I'm sorry."

And then he heard it.

"Zacchaeus, come down, I must stay with you today."

Zacchaeus froze. "He called my name?" he murmured. Tears already falling, he half fell down the tree, desperate to reach the one who had called him so lovingly. How could this be? Scrambling up from the ground, he gazed into Jesus' face. All he could see was kind acceptance, a deep knowing, and love.

Zacchaeus melted. All his pain and anger, his need to crush those who despised him, all disappeared like a dream. Jesus loved him and wanted to be with him. He'd called his name with love. What else could Zacchaeus do but respond and give back the love he'd just received to love the One who loved him?

Extra Readings

Isaiah 43:1-4; Ephesians 1:3-8

Day 22 – The Prayer That Won't be Answered

(1 Kings 19:1-18)

"He came to a broom tree, sat down under it and prayed that he might die. 'I have had enough, Lord' he said. 'Take my life. I am no better than my ancestors.' Then he lay down under the tree and fell asleep."

Depression can hit us with the force of a tsunami, knocking us off our feet and flattening our joy in living. Elijah had just won a mammoth victory against the prophets of Baal, so why wasn't he celebrating the manifest favour of God? Instead he was running for his life because of Jezebel's threats.

Are you experiencing the burn-out of a spiritual high, followed by a crashing low today? Open your heart to God for He loves you so much. Just as Elijah discovered that the Lord was with him – not just in the midst of the victory but when he was full of fear too – so God is with you right now. The clouds may mass together and cover the sun, but the sun is still there and will break through and shine again.

I find it interesting that the angel of the Lord asked Elijah three times "What are you doing here?" The Lord would have known about Jezebel's threats, so He didn't actually need the information. I believe He was giving Elijah the opportunity to share what was weighing him down, which he did parrot fashion, repeatedly trotting out the same story.

It's clear Elijah's mind was fixed on a certain theme, as often happens when we hit a low place. This passage shows that it's important to be real about our struggles when we pray. God knows us inside-out, so we never need to pretend with Him. As Psalm 139:1-4 expresses:

"You have searched me, Lord and you know me. You know when I sit and when I rise. You perceive my thoughts from afar; you discern my going out and my lying down; you are familiar with all my ways."

So, if He already knows us so completely, why do we need to tell Him things? Part of the answer lies in what happens at times like this. Elijah's story shows how easy it is to get sucked down by the situations we are facing, and by our reaction to them. In the desert it can be hard to see any green vegetation, because the hot air sucks everything dry. In times of depression our hearts are like that too, but the roots of our joy are still there – they are just buried. Taking the time to honestly acknowledge our feelings is the equivalent of the winds that sweep over the desert and expose the roots of new growth, giving them the opportunity to grow.

God is not looking for victory at all cost, but transparency and growth. Hiding our feelings may seem like a faith-filled thing to do, but it actually means we are denying our pain not dealing with it. Such denial can work its way deep into our hearts and erode our joy. God wouldn't let Elijah fall into that trap and doesn't want you to either. He asked Elijah, "What are you doing here?" As Elijah answered, God was able to speak into his depression with wisdom and a true understanding. Elijah's perspective changed and he was able to move on from the story that had been crippling him

Reflect

What question is God asking you today?

What will you tell Him?

Listen to Him. What new perspective does He want to give you? Or what steps does He want you to take?

God says:

"Beloved child, I am with you and nothing can separate you from my love. I will never leave you nor forsake you, for you are wholly dear to me. Know that I have chosen you to be my friend and you are in my plan. As you open your heart to me I will make all mysteries known to you."

Extra readings

Psalm 46:1-7; Jonah 3:10; 4:11

Day 23 – In the Darkest Place

(Matthew 26:36-45)

"My soul is overwhelmed with sorrow to the point of death."

Are you in a dark place, struggling to face something too hard to even contemplate? How do you deal with sorrow so devastating that you can barely stand?

Jesus knows.

He knows like no one else could ever know.

He went to Gethsemane and cried out His horror at entering that barren wilderness of sorrow and separation; the weight of sorrow that He was literally dying under.

Jesus knows.

He knows your darkness, your hopelessness and bleakness of heart that can't let in any light.

He knows. For even the light of day turned to darkness as He died.

Jesus went into that wilderness for you.

He loves you.

He is there, with you.

And He is also with you, who have been betrayed. You have unbearable pain, so deep that you cannot even cry, rejection like a knife tearing your heart into splinters.

Jesus knows. He weeps for you.

He carries your pain.

He is there,
with you.

And you who cannot sleep, who feel full of guilt and regret, Jesus loves you. He went to that darkest place for you and literally carried your sins and shame so you could know the peace of forgiveness.

"Because of our sins he was wounded, beaten because of the evil we did. We are healed by the punishment he suffered, made whole by the blows he received." (Isaiah 53:5 GNT)

He is there, with you. Let Him carry that shame. Let Him take your regret.

And you who have been deeply wounded... I now know that Jesus felt my pain when I was crushed by another's sin and made to carry their shame; shame that I falsely believed to be my own.

He took my self-hatred, my disgust at being me. He wept for the sorrow that broke my heart and allowed His own to be broken for me.

Jesus loves you too.

He is there,
with you.

Let Him heal you. Let Him whisper to you that you are beautiful, clean and pure because of Him.

And you, who turn to others for friendship, only to be ignored. You feel alone and are hurting, comfortless in your loneliness.

Jesus knows.

He sought a refuge, but found none.

He longed for the support of His friends, but they fell asleep.

He who healed the sick, comforted the lonely, chose the despised and was there for all, faced the darkest pit of His life alone.

He knows your loneliness and longing for comfort and, unlike His friends who slept at His moment of greatest need, Jesus never sleeps:

"He who watches over you will not slumber. Indeed, He who watches over Israel will neither slumber nor sleep." (Psalm 121:3-4)

Never doubt that there is someone out there who knows what you are feeling.

He entered that darkest place that you might have hope.

He carried your sorrow that you could be comforted.

He took the deepest of rejections that you need never be alone.

He willingly carried your sin to transform your despair into joy.

Reflect

Read this extract from my reflection about Gethsemane:

From deep within you a cry tore its way from your heart.

"Father, yours is the perfect way, yours is the way I choose."

Love poured into your heart. Wave after wave it filled you – the Father's love, your love, the Father's will, your will. Weeping you stretched out your hands to the world that was about to kill you. Whatever the pain, you would carry that blanket of filth and brokenness; you would save those beautiful ones; you would restore them and bring them alive again. The tide of love was so great that you knew it would tear your very body to pour it all out.

"But that is why I came," you said, and calmly, lovingly, you walked to meet your murderers.

Prayer

Thank you, Jesus. I worship you. I thank you from the bottom of my heart for all you gave for me. Help me to receive it in the deepest place in my heart and learn to love you as you love me.

Extra Readings

Psalm 22; 2 Corinthians 5:21

Day 24 – Waiting with Expectation

(Psalm 40:1- 5; 11-13)

"I waited patiently for the Lord. He turned to me and heard my
cry. He lifted me out of the slimy pit, out of the mud and mire.
He set my feet upon a rock and gave me a firm place to stand.
He put a new song in my mouth, a song of praise to our God.
Many will see and fear and put their trust in the Lord."

In our age of instant gratification, waiting can be difficult. I am quite patient, but waiting for the bus, especially when I am carrying heavy shopping, is a great trigger of a Frustrated Bad Mood!

Some types of waiting – like waiting for medical test results or to hear if an application has been successful – can swing us from hope into fear.

Then there is the waiting that's full of joyful anticipation, like looking forward to a long planned holiday.

In Psalm 40 David is waiting patiently. Waiting in this way for the Lord to answer our prayers is a sign of how much we trust Him, even when things don't happen as quickly as we would hope. Patience is an outworking of the peace He gives us. Peace which rests not on our circumstances, but on Him – His faithfulness; His trustworthiness; His commitment to us; His promise to always hear and answer us.

A prophetic word

God is showing me that you have been badly let down by someone you trusted. Your heart is ripped apart and you daren't trust in His commitment. I saw Jesus on the cross, the nails in His hands and feet, His body ripped and scourged. He was looking at you with such compassion and saying,

"I know, beloved child. I carried your pain. I know you are heartbroken, so was I. But dare to trust me even in your brokenness, because I truly am there for you."

A quick prayer...

Lord Jesus, please hold your broken-hearted children in your arms of love. Let them know that you are there for them and are utterly faithful. Amen.

David trusted in the Lord's love. Even though he was in a muddy pit of life-threatening difficulties, he was confident in God's faithfulness. A miry pit is like quicksand, symbolic of the things that suck us down and paralyse us, and David was paralysed. Maybe it was fear or hopelessness? Whatever it was, he couldn't loosen himself from its grip.

Are you there right now? Don't despair, God is with you. His ears hear your cry, just as He heard David. David knew that

God would hear him. Do you know that? Every sigh or cry from your heart matters to Him. He will respond and rescue you, but He does ask that you trust Him; that you wait patiently, knowing that He loves you and is faithful.

Our dogs are a powerful picture of expectancy. Once, they wanted a walk but I was busy. It was hard to ignore them, because they look so appealing when they want something – ears pricked up, heads to one side, big yearning eyes…

I felt bad, but had to finish something first, so I shut the door and went back to work. When I opened it ten minutes later, they were still there, ears pricked, heads to one side, big yearning eyes…

I burst out laughing, hardly believing they had waited so patiently in that same position as when I'd shut the door in their faces. They trusted that their desire would be fulfilled and, of course, it was. I took them out eventually and they were rewarded.

Reflect

God, your Father, wants to bless you and answer your prayers in such a way that He will impact those around you with the beauty of true trust. As David wrote,

"Many will see and fear and put their trust in the Lord."

Will you be someone who infects others with joyful expectation as you choose to trust in God's love and faithfulness?

Extra Readings

1 Samuel 24:1-18 ; Isaiah 40:31

Day 25 – Believing and Receiving His Words

(John 15: 3–11)

"If you remain in me and my words remain in you, ask whatever you wish and it will be done for you."

Thinking again about the fact that listening to negative things can cause parts of our lives to "die", I began to think about the importance of listening to God's words, which are full of life giving truth.

When Jesus was hungry after a forty day fast while in the wilderness, the enemy tempted Him to turn stones into bread. But Jesus replied,

"Man shall not live on bread alone but on every word that comes from the mouth of God." (Matthew 4:4)

Sometimes when I am anxious I start to snack on sweet things. One snack is OK, but going from one to another can cause problems. Why do I do it? For me it's a way of escape from something I am struggling with. It's an immediate source of comfort, but ultimately it can't help or change me and usually adds guilt into the mix too.

Satan wanted Jesus to look for an easy way to satisfy His hunger and we see this same temptation at work today with society emphasising all the material things we "need". But Jesus gets to the heart of our need. Food is important, but to become truly alive we need to be "eating" God's words. Not just the occasional word but, *every word that comes from the mouth of God*"!

How do we feel about that? Do we hear Jesus? To what degree do we receive His words for ourselves? What part do they play in our lives? How important do we consider it to spend time listening to Him? Do we build that time into our daily lives?

As a deaf person, understanding what people say is never automatic. I have to focus on one person at a time, because I can never just casually tune into conversations. I don't hear the general flow of chitchat, so I build my understanding on the few words that someone writes down for me. Those words become very important. I think about them and mull them over and they become a source of further questions.

In a similar way we can listen for God's words and choose to not just skim read, but spend time thinking about them, mulling them over and taking them in. The effects could well be life changing.

Many of us have wounded hearts. When I was first a Christian I had so much emotional pain because of childhood abuse. A friend encouraged me to believe the truth of these words from Isaiah 43:4:

"You are precious and honoured in my sight and … I love you."

They were expressing truths that were the opposite to my feelings about myself, but I tried to believe them and speak them out as God's word of truth. Over the weeks that followed, my wilderness of fear and pain gradually ebbed away as the "knowing" grew within me that I was indeed loved by God. Soon I found myself wanting to comfort and help other hurting people.

Jesus said, *"Remain in me and let my words remain in you."* His words are dynamic and true and therefore more powerful to change and empower us than anything else we could encounter. Satan hates it when we trust in Jesus' words of love because doing so breaks his power to attack us. Let's really believe that God is our true Father, Friend, Brother, Lord and Bridegroom and choose to listen to His voice above all others.

Reflect

Sit in a comfortable chair. Thank Jesus for being with you. Tell Him you love Him and want to hear Him. Slowly and reflectively read Song of Solomon 2:10-14.

Is there any word or phrase that calls out to you? Stay with that phrase, asking Jesus, *"Lord, what are you saying to me through this?"*

Jot down anything that comes to you and ask Him to help you apply His words in your life. Spend some time in thankfulness and worship.

Extra Readings

Psalm 12:6-7; Matthew 17:1-5

Day 26 – In Times of Shipwreck

(Acts 27:1-28:2)

"Last night an angel of the Lord ... stood beside me and said, 'Do not be afraid, Paul, you must stand trial before Caesar and God has graciously given you the lives of all who sail with you.'"

Do you ever feel caught up in a terrifying situation? Maybe God has spoken to you about a particular thing and you've been stepping into that promise, but now tough things are happening and others are making decisions that deeply affect you.

Maybe like Paul you've been in this tough place for a long time and can't imagine how God's promises will ever be fulfilled? God wants to reassure you that,

"I know the plans I have for you, plans to prosper you and not to harm you; plans to give you a hope and a future." (Jeremiah 29:11)

God is watching over you and His plans for you are bigger than you could ever imagine. If a sparrow can't fall to the ground without Him knowing (Matthew 10:29), be assured that He cares about every detail of your life. Nothing happens by chance with God and nothing is ever wasted.

This closing story in Acts reveals the wonder of God's plans for us, which stand strong, even when our lives seem to be shipwrecked. Paul has been a prisoner for over two years and now, together with many other prisoners, is sailing to Rome under guard. They are in God's plan, but then the weather turns against them and Paul knows that *our voyage is going to be disastrous and bring great loss to ship and cargo and to our own lives.*

Despite this warning, those in charge choose to press on with the journey. Then they are caught in the maelstrom of Hurricane Northeaster and despite all their efforts the ship begins to break apart.

"(They) finally give up all hope of being saved."

How did Paul react when his voice went unheard to such terrible effect? How do you react? When I am not listened to I sometimes feel enraged, a deep pain coming from my childhood years and unhealed elements of being deaf. I am tempted to give up on my faith, but God calls me, as He did Paul, to draw close to Him and listen for His voice.

As Paul prayed, even amidst all the chaos and terror of the storm, God spoke into His heart telling him not to be afraid because *"you must stand trial before Caesar and God has graciously given you the lives of all who sail with you."*

God's plan was not just for Paul, but *every* person on that ship.

That goes for you and me too.

Many of us feel insignificant, but the Bible clearly shows that we are each uniquely created by God to become like Jesus and to do His works. He will use *all* that we experience in life to help us grow in His love and grace. I would never have chosen to be abused or to struggle with deafness, and God did not cause these things to happen any more than he caused Paul's ship to be wrecked. But He carries us in our traumas and works through them to bring us closer to Him and prepare us for our unique calling. Throughout that terrible shipwreck, God encouraged and empowered Paul, who then encouraged the men. When they eventually ran aground in Malta, they saw that God was truly with them in the incredible kindness they received.

Reflect

Will you let God hold you in your time of shipwreck and grow and nurture you into His amazing purposes for your life?

Prayer

Father, I've felt so broken, but thank you that you are holding me and have a wonderful plan for me. I choose to come to you in the midst of the chaos and listen for your voice of love. Amen.

Extra Readings

1 Peter 2:9-10; James 1:2-4

Day 27 – The Lord Is Near

(Philippians 4:4–9)

"Rejoice in the Lord always. I will say it again, rejoice. Let your gentleness be evident to all. The Lord is near. Do not be anxious about anything, but in everything, by prayer and petition, with thanksgiving, present your requests to God. And the peace of God which transcends all understanding will guard your hearts and your minds in Christ Jesus."

Is it really possible to always be rejoicing? Wouldn't that make me a bit irritating? Surely I'd just come over as an eternal optimist who always looks on the bright side and never acknowledges any struggles? Is that what Paul is actually saying?

"Rejoice in the Lord always."

Rejoice – in the Lord – always.

Not, *always rejoice…*

But, *rejoice – in the Lord – always.*

If the focus of our rejoicing is "in the Lord" rather than a perpetual rejoicing, it becomes far more attainable. Paul is asking us to develop hearts of thankfulness and the willingness to affirm who the Lord is, His goodness, faithfulness and love.

That means I'm still allowed to be sad, confused, afraid… I just need to choose to rejoice in who the Lord is at the same time.

Have you made time today to notice the Lord's goodness?

Why not take a few moments now, because that word "always" means being willing to lift our hearts up to the Lord at any time, even in the middle of a difficult day. He will give us eyes to see His goodness if we are willing to look.

Recently, God has been speaking to me about my anxiety. Paul tells us not to be anxious about *anything*. There are so many things we *do* get anxious about. I often worry that a meal I am cooking won't turn out well or a haircut will go wrong. Then there are the serious worries: a friend who is ill; another friend struggling emotionally; financial concerns. So many potential worries for us all. How can we not be anxious?

But as I meditated on these verses I discovered the key in one little phrase. In fact, it's the phrase that starts off Paul's exhortation not to worry. He says very simply, *"The Lord is near."* The Lord is near us. He is standing alongside us in all we have to deal with, ready to give strength, peace, love and joy. He knows the nitty-gritty of our lives, the harsh reality of how things can change in a moment.

Yesterday, I was emptying a rubbish bag and it split as I pushed back the door to get to the outside bin. Kitchen waste and cat litter spilled all over the porch and front steps! Something heavy flew backwards and shattered a window and fragments of glass added themselves to the mix. I fetched a dustpan, brush and disinfectant, feeling fed up. But as I knelt in the rubbish, I suddenly became aware of Jesus kneeling with me. He didn't care about getting dirty, He was just loving me in the midst of everything – just as He is always with you too. He was saying,

"I've taken every trace of muck from your life. All you worry about, I care about, and have already worked out on your behalf. Every little detail, every tiny fragment of pain, regret or worry I've carried in my great love for you. Be at peace, I am near and I will never forsake you."

Reflect

That prophetic word of love from the Lord is for you as much as it was for me. Spend a few minutes reflecting on the words and allowing the Spirit to bring God's peace and comfort into your heart.

Prayer

Lord Jesus, thank you that you are always with us, and as we listen you give us true peace and comfort. Help us in our anxieties to rest in your love and even when things seem a complete mess, to know you are there, kneeling in the midst of it with us. With you alongside us, we can be full of joy. Amen.

Extra Readings

Isaiah 9:1-3; 6-7; Psalm 92:1-5

Day 28 – When Anxiety Hits, Be Confident

(2 Kings 6:13-18; Proverbs 3:5)

"'Don't be afraid,' the prophet answered. 'Those who are with us are more than those who are with them.'"

"Trust in the Lord with all your heart and lean not on your own understanding."

Anxiety makes us feel paralysed and helpless. We all get anxious, but the Lord wants us to have a new perspective; to see from Heaven's viewpoint, not just our own.

In 2 Kings 6 we are confronted with two very different reactions to the same situation: anxiety and confidence.

Elisha and his servant were in extreme danger because the king of Aram was enraged at how, through divine revelation, Elisha kept thwarting his plans to attack the king of Israel. Eventually, the king of Aram sent a great force of chariots and horses to where he'd heard Elisha was based.

"They went by night and surrounded the city."

I find the word "surrounded" significant, because Satan's attacks often make us feel surrounded on all sides and helpless to know what to do to resolve the situation. Hopelessness and defeat sneak their way into our hearts and we feel the enemy has already won.

"When the servant of the man of God got up ... the next morning, an army with horses and chariots had surrounded the city. 'Oh no, my Lord, what shall we do?' the servant asked."

As far as he was concerned, they were already staring death in the face and for him that was the only reality.

But actually, it wasn't reality.

It's true that the enemy was there in terrifying numbers, but there was a greater reality that meant the difference between his anxiety and Elisha's confidence.

"'Don't be afraid,' the prophet answered. 'Those who are with us are more than those who are with them.'"

Through the revelation of the Spirit, Elisha saw the reality of the kingdom of Heaven and knew with a heart confidence that God's power and the hosts of Heaven were so much greater than that of any earthly king.

Can we have such confidence?

Proverbs 3:5 (AMP) is very illuminating:

"Lean on, trust in, and be confident in the Lord with all your

heart and mind and do not rely on your own insight or under-standing."

Think of that word "confident".

Confidence is a very attractive quality. A confident person inspires a positive feeling, even in the most anxious hearts. Confidence is a smile and a peaceful heart. It is the ability to take a step without needing to anxiously go over all the details. A confident person can face their own limitations and still trust that they can achieve something amazing.

Am I confident? Sometimes! But this verse is calling me not just to be confident, but to be *confident in God* which is a different ask. God wants me to trust in and rely on Him, not on myself. I may feel weak, but with my God I can climb a mountain and stand firm against the enemy's attacks.

Will I let my very weakness become a stepping stone of trust in God's power? Elisha, seeing that God's forces were so much mightier, was able to pray for his servant to see with spiritual, rather than earthly vision. The Bible says that the servant then, *"saw the hills full of horses and chariots of fire all around Elisha."*

It's so exciting that the servant was enabled to see like Elisha. I want my confidence to be rooted in God and to have that same peace and trust that will draw others out of anxiety into God-given confidence. I want to live trusting in the Lord, seeing every wall and mountain as climbable with Him.

Reflect

It is a wonderful thing that the Lord gave Himself for us that our confidence need never rest on ourselves but on Him. Is your confidence resting in the Lord? If not, ask Him to give you a fresh vision of His love and power.

Prayer

Forgive me, Lord, for every time I've tried to trust in myself and walked in anxiety as a result. I choose to see with your eyes today and put my confidence in you.

Extra Readings

Acts 3:1-10; Psalm 18:27-33

Day 29 – When the World is Against You

(Exodus 2:14-15)

"The man said, 'who made you ruler and judge over us? Are you thinking of killing me as you killed the Egyptian?' Then Moses was afraid and thought, 'What I did must have become known.' When Pharaoh heard of this he tried to kill Moses, but Moses fled from Pharaoh and went to live in Midian."

Imagine Moses' heartache in life. A near death experience as a baby; rescue from a watery grave; the confusion of being brought up in a culture not his own; killing someone; rejection from his own people; the threat of murder by his adopted grandfather.

No wonder Moses ran away.

I did the same thing once because I couldn't cope with life anymore after years of abuse and struggle. One little negative word lit a fuse and all the buried rejection and fear exploded. I ran away leaving behind all that I knew. I wanted to hide from all the negatives, so they couldn't control me anymore.

I thought I could run from God too, but I discovered I couldn't. He was still with me, even though I was full of rage. He was still with Moses too and ultimately revealed Himself to him.

How about you? Are you running away too?

Sometimes life gets overwhelming and like Moses we do something crazy. Is that where you are now, in a place you never expected to be? Have your family rejected you or do you feel that the world is against you? Are you struggling with something you've done that has backfired?

Moses reacted like many of us do and withdrew from the life he'd been living. He chose to exile himself in Midian where he married the daughter of a Midianite priest and became a shepherd. Acts 7:30 says that Moses was in Midian for 40 years. What a huge chunk of his life wasted.

But was it wasted? As we explore Exodus 2-3 we discover some amazing truths. Firstly, God was always with Moses, even though he had made a mess of things. God never abandoned him, nor did He give up on the plans He had for him. Instead He told Moses,

"...the cry of the Israelites has reached me ... So now go. I am sending you to Pharaoh to bring my people the Israelites out of Egypt." (Exodus 3:9-10)

When Moses protested, overwhelmed by his sense of inadequacy, God's answer was, *"I will be with you."*

God wanted to reassure Moses of His constant presence with him. He knew his daily rituals, including where Moses would

When the World is Against You

be taking the sheep that day. He also wanted Moses to know that his years on the run would not be wasted because they had given him invaluable experience of the desert and of being in charge of a vast group (albeit sheep!)

So Moses discovered that God would use even his mistakes and traumas to make him all that he needed to be. His desert became a holy place of passion and encounter with God.

Reflect

Think about your life, the good and bad times, the achievements and the mistakes. If you've been running away, ask God to reveal His presence with you. Ask Him to transform your desert into a place of passion and holy encounter. Listen for His voice. What is He saying to you?

God says:

"I am with you child. I will never give up on you. Even when you go wrong I am for you not against you. Never forget that I have called and chosen you."

Extra Readings

Psalm 139; Acts 9:1-19

133

Day 30 – A Heavenly Visitation

(Luke 2:8–20)

"An angel of the Lord appeared to them and the glory of the Lord shone around them and they were terrified. But the angel said to them: 'Do not be afraid, I bring you good news that will cause great joy for all the people.'"

Many wildernesses are brought about by major difficulties in our lives, but one that we all experience day in and day out, is *routine*.

Routine: those mundane aspects of life; the chores that always need doing; keeping house; looking after the family; going to work; grocery shopping…

Some of us live more spontaneously, but even if you're a renowned actor, your daily life will be full of packing suitcases, learning lines, staying at yet another hotel...

How does God want to transform the routine of our lives?

This story focuses on the shepherds. They were rough sleepers, wild looking men, uneducated and lacking in social skills. Their job was essential, but not one that people respected.

On this particular night they were out in the fields keeping watch over their flocks. These fields were vast barren areas of grass and rocks. It was a battle to find water and good pasture. It could be dangerous with the wild animals.

The hours ticked by, this night like any other.

Do you feel your days are like that?

One day passing to the next?

Are you in a wilderness of routine?

For the shepherds, that wilderness was suddenly shattered. An angel broke through the dark nothingness of the night sky and a dazzling light shone all around them.

"They were terrified."

When God shows us His glory it is awesome.

I was once in our local recreation ground walking Marilyn's guide dog. It was a routine job and the field was very boring. It was a cold, miserable day and I just wanted to get round it as quickly as possible. Suddenly, a ray of sun broke through the clouds and turned the entire muddy field to gold.

I stood frozen as everything took on an unearthly stillness. I knew this wasn't just the sun coming out, this was God. He was there revealing His glory.

Why he'd chosen to do so, I didn't know, but a verse from Romans 8 dropped into my mind:

"Creation waits in eager expectation for the sons of God to be revealed."

Then He said,

"Just as this ordinary field turned gold when the sun shone upon it, so my sons and daughters are carriers of my glory. This very world is waiting for my children to rise up as my beloved ones, knowing the fullness of my resources and flowing with my love."

I was overcome by this encounter with God and how He used the very ordinary elements of my walk to bring heaven to earth. In a moment my routine job was transformed into a holy encounter and I received a message that has shaped my perspective ever since.

God had good news to share with the shepherds which He wanted the whole world to know about: the birth of His son.

His angelic hosts were full of worship and joy, but He wanted us to be part of that celebration too.

He chose the shepherds to be the first to hear His good news.

Why the shepherds? Why *not* the shepherds?

And why did God choose me?

The answer is that He is in the centre of our "ordinary" and longs to give us glimpses into Heaven. He said to Jeremiah,

"Call to me and I will answer you and tell you great and unsearchable things you do not know." (Jeremiah 33:3)

Reflect

After the shepherds had been to Bethlehem and discovered baby Jesus in the stable with Mary and Joseph, Scripture says,

"The shepherds returned, glorifying and praising God for all the things they had heard and seen which were just as they had been told."

What effect did their encounter with the angelic hosts have on the shepherds?

What effect might such an encounter have on me?

Prayer

Lord, open my eyes that I might see.

Extra Readings

Luke 1:26-38; Ephesian 1:16-23

Day 31 – I Have Seen the Lord

(John 20:10-18)

"Mary Magdalene went to the disciples with the news, 'I have seen the Lord.'"

Two friends recently lost loved ones and I sent them messages expressing God's comfort. But as I wrote their cards I thought, what does that comfort look like when you are grieving for the one who made your world go round? How terrible that loss is, with all the memories of happy times together and those shattering moments, now they've died, when you realise things will never be the same again. How can we experience any sense of well-being?

The pain of missing someone we love is acute, especially if they died suddenly or tragically. And yet, in God there *is* true comfort. As Christians we know they are with the Lord and gloriously free from all pain and suffering. Yes, we miss them, but we rejoice, knowing that one day there will be a most amazing reunion. The promise of resurrection must never be downplayed because that strips the good news from the Gospel. Jesus died to forgive us and rose from the dead so that we would all be able to receive His wonderful promise of eternal life.

Those mourning Jesus' death had not only lost their loved one in the most horrific way, but their hopes and dreams had been totally smashed in the process. They knew He was the Messiah, so how could it have ended like this?

Like Mary in this story, we can be so full of pain that it feels like there is no way through. Mary could only stand at the tomb and weep. She didn't even register the fact that she had spoken with two angels and didn't recognise Jesus when she first saw Him. As she gazed into the emptiness of the tomb, her heart just kept crying, "He's gone!"

Grief can blind us to God's love, but Jesus is always there. He may come to us in such ordinary guise that, like Mary, we fail to recognise Him. But as we keep looking and listening He will speak to us and minister healing to our hearts.

It is telling that Jesus asked Mary, *"Woman why are you crying?"* He knew why she was crying, but He wanted her to talk to Him about it. When pain overwhelms us, we sometimes just need to talk with someone. Putting words to our turmoil opens the door to letting those feelings go. When Jesus went on to whisper Mary's name in that old loving way, she heard and suddenly recognition dawned.

"She turned towards him and cried out in Aramaic, Rabboni..."

From devastation and mourning to joy and exhilaration: the wonderful fruit of resurrection.

Today, are you standing before a tomb of lost hopes and shattered dreams? Open your eyes to see Jesus – He is there with you and will never forsake you. Share your heart with

Him. He is listening. He understands. Now hear Him whisper your name.

God says:

"My child, I am your comfort and strength. Do not be afraid, for my mercy is beyond imagining. Be at rest and know you will be reunited. In that day there will be no end to your joy. Let me open your eyes to the treasure of my promises and the beauty that brings you my healing: the hug of a friend, a flower opening its buds, the sweetness of birdsong, and those rainbow memories of special moments together. I love you and am always with you to share your tears and to give you gifts of joy."

Prayer

Lord Jesus, thank you that in your love, you bring victory over death and despair. Open my eyes to see you, even in the midst of ordinary things. Open my ears to hear you and my heart to receive your joy. Amen.

Extra Readings

John 16:16-22; Psalm 30:11

Day 32 – Pressing On

(Philippians 3:12-14)

"Not that I have already obtained all this, or have already been made perfect, but I press on to take hold of that for which Christ Jesus took hold of me ... Forgetting what is behind and straining towards what is ahead I press on towards the goal to win the prize for which Christ has called me heavenwards in Christ Jesus."

I have a friend who is coping with many health needs in her family and suffers with depression herself. I admire her so much for the way she keeps holding onto the Lord. Her life journey is passing through harsh terrain and many of us are on a similar path. God wants to encourage us today to press on with hope into all that He has for us.

This passage inspires us to live to win the heavenly prize which Christ has set before us: our kingdom calling.

Paul says he is *"forgetting what is behind."* He is not worrying about his past, as that is already covered by the blood of Christ. There were so many things that could have held Paul back, especially the potentially crippling regret of the terrible things he had done to the new church. In other letters, Paul describes himself as the worst of sinners, so he obviously understands the horror of his actions. Yet, he refuses to be chained by regret or to let it stop him moving forward. He knows that Christ has taken hold of him and that is true for you and me too.

The whole reason for the cross was that Jesus took our past regrets, failures, shame, fear and hurt. We are ALL called heavenward and all have a prize specially created for us in God's love. We ALL have a destiny to fulfil that He longs for us to move into, step-by-step, in the power of His love and grace.

In 2008 I was turned down for ordination training after following what I believed was God's calling. I was sure I had heard Him correctly and was stunned when it didn't happen. The rejection tapped into previous "failures", like when I'd had to give up teacher training because of my deafness. In my mind, the ordination rejection proved that I was a failure and couldn't hear the Lord. Deep down, I was constantly looking back, not moving on. I stopped writing, stopped seeking for specific prophetic words and drifted in many other areas of my true gifting. It has been a desert path, but God is now graciously freeing me. Books are on the go again and other new ideas. But it is very sad that I took 8 years to start pressing into my heavenly destiny again. Wonderfully, I know God has still been using me, sometimes in amazing ways, but I don't want to let false feelings of failure define me anymore.

Just as I am in Christ's hands, so are you. He loves you and has a plan that is just right for you. Even if you do make mistakes, His blood covers them. He has chosen you and is calling you heavenwards. Looking back will do nothing but rob you of joy. Pressing on may be challenging at times and make you take steps you couldn't have imagined taking, but the joy you experience will be amazing – the joy of being in the centre of His loving purposes.

If Paul could press into that despite his sin, then so can we.

Reflect

What do you think your heavenly prize is?

Do you know your calling?

Take some time to talk with Him about the feelings these questions evoke.

Prayer

Father, thank you that you love me and have chosen me. Forgive me for disregarding the power of your forgiveness and your sacrifice on the cross for me. I choose today to fix my eyes upon you, Lord Jesus, and to press on to take hold of all you have for me. Amen.

Extra Readings

Jeremiah 29:11-14; John 21:15-17

Day 33 – When in Deep Distress

(Psalm 18:6-19)

"In my distress I called to the Lord; I cried to my God for help. From His temple He heard my voice; my cry came before Him, into His ears ... He reached down from on high and took hold of me; he drew me out of deep waters ... He brought me out into a spacious place; he rescued me because he delighted in me."

Are you struggling today? God is there for you and wants to help you.

Can we really trust in His care when we are going through deep distress?

Distress is a big word, describing those raw painful feelings like grief, fear, anger and helplessness. It can hit us out of the blue for the most mundane reasons, or imprison us in despair –especially if, like David, we feel alone and that no one understands or cares.

David was distressed because of Saul, a father figure he had loved and served, but who was jealous of David and determined to kill him. So great was David's anguish that in his efforts to escape, he literally fled into the wilderness seeking refuge amongst the rocks and caves. But nowhere was safe. Even the mightiest rocks couldn't hide him from Saul.

Maybe you too are in a rocky wilderness of pain and feel there is no one you can turn to? David shows us a key: *"In my distress I called to the Lord; I cried to my God for help."*

I can find it hard to genuinely call on the Lord when distress hits me. I feel more like throwing things, weeping, or screaming. I may need to express those emotions and God knows that, but like David, I need to call on the Lord too. He alone truly understands my pain and can help me, even transform me.

I love David's assurance, even in the midst of his pain, that God would hear his cry; that his situation mattered to God and He would respond. This is true for us too. Our prayers and cries of distress matter to Him more than we can ever imagine. If you read the whole psalm you see how dramatically David describes God's anger on his behalf as He hurtles from Heaven to help him. He finishes this section with the words, *"He rescued me because he delighted in me."*

Reflect

God wants you to know today that He delights in you and cares deeply for all your pain. He hears your smallest whisper of a prayer and your loudest scream of distress. He delights in you and loves being with you. He longs to comfort you and act in His holy anger and justice on your behalf. Dare to cry out to Him in your distress today and see how He responds.

Prayer

Father, I feel so distressed today and don't know what to do. I cry out to you, please help me. Thank you that you are with me and want to comfort and strengthen me. You alone can truly work things out for me and I choose to trust you. Amen.

Extra Readings

Isaiah 63:9; Psalm 46:1; John 14:27

Day 34 – When the Brook Dries Up

(1 Kings 17:1-16)

"Some time later the brook dried up because there had been no rain in the land."

My lovely writer friend Emily Owen recently sent me an article she'd written about this story and it was very inspiring. With her permission I will quote from it later.

The setting is a brook. A brook is a small stream that has connotations wrapped around it of happiness, peace, refreshment, safety, fun, friendship and harmony.

The Lord had directed Elijah to a brook and it proved a wonderful source of refreshment during the severe famine. The ravens brought him food and he drank from the brook. How wonderful!

Have you known the joy of the Lord's rich care? I sometimes experience it when travelling on public transport. With my deafness, sight and balance problems it can be tricky, but the Lord takes care of me through lovely fellow travellers offering help. The Lord loves to bless us, but following Jesus can be costly too and He doesn't cocoon us from problems. Instead, He calls us to obey as a sign of our love, and promises great joy as we choose to follow Him whatever the cost.

Elijah was experiencing God's blessing, but then the brook dried up. The famine that was a direct result of his prophecies against Ahab's sin, was now personally affecting him.

How did Elijah feel in that moment? Had God turned His back on him?

Remember, Elijah was alone in the wilderness. When we are isolated it's very easy for the enemy to get in and attack us.

Are you feeling isolated today and wondering what on earth God is doing in your life? Has something happened and knocked you for six? God is with you in all His gentleness and care. He says,

"Be still [beloved child] and know that I am God." (Psalm 46:10)

So Elijah was being blessed, then suddenly, nothing – no more water. Where had it gone? He was thirsty! How could he drink if the brook had dried up?

Emily says in her article, "Perhaps some of us feel like that. That we're satisfied, and life is good, and then something changes. Our brook dries up. There's no more water."

What is that dry brook for you? Your diagnosis of illness? Your ministry suddenly hit by major problems? Your longed-for baby born with a disability?

Whatever the cause, a dry brook is a scary experience, especially because of the confusion it engenders about the reality of God's love.

Emily continues:

"I've experienced many 'dry brooks', one of which was when I lost my hearing at the age of 21. Unlike Elijah, I sat by my dry brook for a long time. It was a time during which God patiently sat with me and, very gently, prepared me to move on … As I turned from my dry brook, I began writing books, something I'd never thought of doing before the brook ran dry.

Perhaps, when we enter dry seasons, God is calling us to move on into something new with Him. But He won't run ahead, He'll patiently sit with us until the time comes when we're ready to move on."[2]

Reflect

Emily talks of sitting by her dry brook. Can you sit for a while like she did? Not rushing to move on, not trying to escape, but just quietly sitting there in all your loss and brokenness?

Can you see the Lord there, patiently sitting with you?

Take your time. Rest in Him. Maybe He will whisper to you. Maybe He will just hold you.

God says:

"Those who trust in the Lord will find new strength. They will soar high on wings like eagles. They will run and not grow weary. They will walk and not faint." (Isaiah 40:31 NLT)

Prayer

Thank you, Father, for being with me. Please help me to rest in your love. Hold me close and when the time is right help me to move on. Amen.

Extra Readings

John 7:37; Psalm 34: 4-10

---

2. Emily Owen, Author and Speaker. This extract was taken from an article Emily contributed to Hearing Eye Magazine, Open Ears, April 2019. Emily became totally deaf at 21 through the condition NF2. You can read her inspiring story in her memoir *Still Emily* which was published in 2016 by Malcolm Down. Emily has also written several devotional books for Authentic Media, the latest of which, *God's Calling Cards*, released in September 2019.

Day 35 – Beloved in the Lord

(Deuteronomy 33:12)

"Let the beloved of the Lord rest secure in Him, for He shields him all day long, and the one the Lord loves rests between His shoulders."

Do you know you are beloved to the Lord? Do you know He never stops thinking about you and loves to spend time with you? Do you know that Jesus went to the cross so that you could know the joy and wonderful security of being loved with an everlasting love by your Heavenly Father?

This knowing is the surest way of seeing our wilderness transformed into beautiful life.

Yesterday, I had an email from a dear friend who is heartbroken because of the ongoing rejection she experiences from her dad. Even though she perseveres in trying to love him, he persists in ignoring her, constantly cutting her off and belittling her, even refusing to look at her.

As I read her email and took in her words, I felt her deep anguish in my own heart. I prayed for her and this beautiful verse from Deuteronomy came to mind and I knew our loving

Heavenly Father felt her pain and longed to comfort her and bring her into a place of security, belonging and belovedness, drawing her to rest in His love.

This is His heart for you and me too. He is a true Father and Friend. He looks upon you with delight. He dances with joy over your achievements. He honours you and loves your uniqueness. You touch His heart with your love for Him and He never stops thinking about you and wanting to bless you. When you are sad He feels your pain and longs to comfort you. Through His Spirit you can know that comfort and hear His words of love bringing healing and affirmation to your heart.

So many of us struggle with the agony of rejection and it can cripple us emotionally. But let's choose today to look into the face of our true Father God who promises He will never leave us nor forsake us (Hebrews 13:5). His Son, Jesus was rejected by so many: His friends, family, even His beloved Father turning away from Him as He hung in agony on the cross.

"My God, my God, why have you forsaken me?" He cried. His anguish is beyond our imagining because He and the Father were one and He was always totally yielded and open to the Father's love. We all sin and to some degree are all inwardly hardened, since from childhood we put up protective walls around our hearts which can stop us feeling so deeply. But Jesus willingly took that full agony of abandonment for you and me. He understands and feels our pain like no other ever can. He heals the broken hearted by pouring His committed, faithful love into our wounds of heartache and loss. He holds us close. He quiets us with His love and rejoices over us with singing (Zephaniah 3:14–17).

Reflect

How does it make you feel, reading that verse in Deuteronomy, that God calls you His beloved?

Do you know that inner security and rest that the verse refers to? If not, ask the Lord to show you what may be robbing you of that beautiful gift. If any hurtful memories come to mind, simply tell Him that you want to give them to Him to deal with.

Thank Him for all the ways He shows His love to you, as expressed in those verses from Zephaniah 3:14-17.

Prayer

Father, thank you for your care and deep love for us. Thank you that you are a hands-on Daddy and a true committed Friend. Please pour the warmth of your love into every hurting place in my heart today. Minister your peace and speak your words of healing, so that I can know that I am your Beloved. Amen.

Extra Readings

Romans 8:35-39; 1 John 3:1

Day 36 – Transforming Faith

(Daniel 2:1–28)

"There is a God in heaven who reveals mysteries."

I love the simplicity of this answer given by Daniel to King Nebuchadnezzar when he needed a magician to interpret his bad dream. Daniel then proceeded to tell the king what he had seen in his dream and what that dream meant.

There is a God in heaven who reveals mysteries.

As a deaf person, everything that is said is a mystery to me unless someone writes it down. I can sit in a room with conversations going on right next to me, but have no idea what they are. I love to ask questions and when someone tells me what's going on I am overjoyed!

God wants to give us that same joy.

It seems an awesome and incredible thing that we have a God who loves to reveal mysteries to us.

Have you experienced Him revealing a mystery to you?

Ask Him today to start to give you new insight and revelation.

Daniel and his friends were captives in Babylon, a spiritual wilderness. They had been picked for a special purpose, to enter the king's service. They would be trained for three years and would be given special food and wine from the king's table. In other words, the king wanted to take all that had been endowed on them by God and make them serve him instead, with all their intellect, physical perfection and great abilities.

It is unlikely that any of us will ever be in quite the same situation, but we can become surrounded by people whose values are totally different to ours; those with no faith or understanding of God and no respect for our faith.

None of my family are Christians, for example, and many of us work in aggressive or intimidating environments. We daily have the choice: how will I react when my colleagues/family are swearing, talking about sex or impure relationships, or want me to go along with some work ethic that is opposed to my faith?

Will I speak out? Will I hide behind a polite smile but never really connect? Or will I forget my faith until I'm in church again when I can resurrect it?

Daniel and his friends could so easily have lost their faith, feeling that God had abandoned them. Instead they determined to trust in Him and refused to compromise their faith in this hostile culture.

"But Daniel resolved not to defile himself with the royal food and wine."

Remember, this was no easy decision because their elite group was very close to the king, who was notorious for his furious temper and swift and murderous judgements.

But God was with them, both in their hearts and within the situation itself.

"God had caused the official to show favour and compassion to Daniel."

God was working in that official's heart and he must have been able to see something different in Daniel's demeanour, actions and way of speaking. Daniel's choice to cultivate the presence of God within him, even though he was far from his own land, was having a huge impact.

God is with us in the hostile environments we find ourselves in and through us wants to touch those around us. He gave Daniel wisdom to know how to respond to the official's natural fear. That same wisdom manifested itself when Nebuchadnezzar, in a furious rage that no one could tell him what he had dreamt, decreed that all his wise men would die.

"Daniel spoke to (the king's officer) with wisdom and tact."

And once Daniel had found out the facts he prayed, asking God to give them revelation so that no one needed to die.

Reflect

Are you trusting in God and giving Him honour in your daily encounters like Daniel did? Or are you more afraid of what others will think if you stand out as being different?

Response

Wisdom

Love

Tact

Prayer

These are all tools of our partnership with God. Will we use them in response to the difficult situations we face and let God's love have an impact on those around us?

Prayer

Thank you, Lord, for these tools of my partnership with you. Help me to use them in response to the difficult situations I face and may your love shine through me to touch those around me. Amen.

Extra Readings

Psalm 84; Acts 16:16-40

Day 37 – Build and Pray

(Jeremiah 29:1-9)

"Also seek the peace and prosperity of the city to which I have carried you into exile. Pray to the Lord for it."

Do you know that right where you are, God wants to use you to bring His blessing?

This is an exciting and challenging chapter as we talk about how we choose to react in the various situations we find ourselves in. Sometimes my reactions can be so me-centred and I just focus on how I am feeling, what I need to be doing and how I expect God to work for me!

I wonder if God scratches His head sometimes and mutters to Jesus, " I thought Tracy became a Christian to follow me, but it seems I'm meant to be following her!"

Sometimes our prayers do have that undertone of wanting God to satisfy our every whim and meet our every need, but He is looking much more for a partnership with us than a shopping list of requests. In Charismatic circles there is a lot of emphasis on God bringing spiritual breakthrough and our need to claim the fulfilment of His promises. God definitely has times and seasons to bring His plans to holy fruition and in some of the prophetic writings, like Isaiah, we get glimpses of Him orchestrating an amazing transformation, brought about by us praying in partnership with Him. For example, in Acts 12 when Peter was put in prison, the church were earnestly praying for him when suddenly an angel appeared in the cell, woke Peter up, supernaturally unlocked his chains and led him to safety! The fact that the church was praying was key to Peter's breakthrough from captivity to freedom.

Has God given you promises that you are waiting for Him to fulfil?

Is this the time and season for your breakthrough? Or does He want to carry out a maturing work in your life at this time, empowering you to be a holy influencer where you are?

In today's reading, the Israelites had been taken into exile by King Nebuchadnezzar. God had warned this would happen if they didn't return to Him, but they'd refused to listen or change their ways. They continued to sin, worshipping false gods and practising ungodly ways.

So now Jeremiah's prophecies have come true and they've been taken into exile. Because of false prophets the people are on tenterhooks waiting for their release, but God had already decreed the exile would last for seventy years. He needed to work in His peoples' hearts, since they had gone so far from Him. Yes, He would bring them out of captivity, but He needed them to listen and work in partnership with Him first. He wanted them to bring a holy influence on the land they were now in; to put down roots and establish themselves there. I believe He was saying that as they literally planted seeds and dug gardens in the middle of this spiritual wilderness, they would be planting seeds of His love and power too.

He also told them to pray:

"Seek the peace and prosperity of the city to which I have carried you."

How awesome that when we find ourselves in a hostile situation we have the power of God through our prayers to change the very atmosphere. I remember once, sitting in a park with Marilyn and another friend and having a prayer time together. Suddenly God spoke in my heart saying,

"Do you realise I am touching all who pass by with my love as you pray?"

I was shocked as I hadn't even noticed other people and certainly wasn't praying for them. God said,

"Every time you pray together, the very ground becomes sacred and as others walk through it I can touch them with my love."

Reflect

Spend some time with the Lord reflecting on this passage and ask Him how He wants to use you as a holy influencer where you are.

Extra Readings

Jeremiah 29:10-14; Mark 5:18-20

Day 38 – In You I Take Refuge

(Psalm 16)

"Keep me safe, O God, for in you I take refuge."

I was reading this psalm today and stopped short at the first verse. David said to the Lord, *"In you I take refuge."*

In the Bible, fortresses and refuges were essential. People needed to know where to run to when danger threatened, so a refuge was a place of protection and concealment. In modern times we talk about places that are a refuge from, for example, natural disasters, stress and abuse. A friend with an amazing vision to help families runs a Christian refuge which is a beautiful bungalow filled with God's love. Over the years, many families have sought refuge there and found God's help.

We all need something or someone to turn to when life gets tough.

Recently, the news featured the ongoing war in Yemen with traumatised children hiding behind broken walls as yet more bombs fell. Their country is literally war torn with no safe places left.

Where can such children find refuge? Is that the kind of refuge you need?

When I was a child I often tried to hide in my bed. I imagined that if I submerged myself completely under the blankets, with not even the top of my head showing, I would be invisible. I would lie perfectly still, cocooned by both the blankets and the false belief that they could keep me safe.

Are you feeling unsafe or vulnerable like that?

Many turn to other sources of "protection", but just as my blanket cocoon couldn't keep me safe, neither can multiple relationships, busyness or drugs.

"In you I take refuge."

What do I take refuge in when I am struggling or afraid? Do I turn to the Lord and trust Him to help me? Or do I turn to other things? I would love to say that I always turn to the Lord, but deep down I know that often it is other things or people that I shelter behind when I am afraid.

Are you afraid today? Do you need a refuge like David's?

David experienced great fear as he fled to remote locations to hide from Saul. But although he hid in literal caves, he still needed to take refuge in the Lord to find true peace.

What is that refuge in the Lord? Is it something we can all find?

The key to finding it is shown in David's words:

"In you, *I take refuge.*"

It is being in God's presence, acknowledging He is there with me, and choosing to trust Him and believe He wants to help me and is on my side.

In that place of rest in God's presence, David was able to be real about his fears.

He trusted in the Lord's protection and care.

He listened for guidance and received God's peace

He was able to say,

"I will praise the Lord who counsels me; even at night my heart instructs me. I keep my eyes always on the Lord, with him at my right hand I will not be shaken."

Do you know that peace? God longs to be our refuge and enable us to grow in our inner strength and depth of trust. When He is our refuge, rather than the people or things around us, we can receive revelation about our situation and God's ever present faithfulness and power.

Reflect

While I often turn to friends for their support or escape into books, their help is only temporary. They can't replace the Lord as my source of inner strength.

Who or what is my refuge today?

Who or what is yours?

Is there anything you've been turning to that you know now is a false security?

Offer it to the Lord and ask Him to help you to put your trust in Him.

Read the rest of this psalm and let God speak to you.

God says:

"You are the apple of my eye. I love you with an everlasting love. Come to me and find rest, rest for your soul."

Extra Readings

Psalm 23; Psalm 31

Day 39 – A Father's Joy

(Luke 15:11-32)

"But while he was still a long way off, his father saw him and was filled with compassion for him. He ran to his son, threw his arms around him and kissed him."

Oh the joy and pathos of this story about the wilderness of a family broken apart: the Father who never gives up loving; the younger son who messes up and returns home feeling worthless; and the older brother with a slave mentality.

It so fits what we see in society today, with our broken families, fatherlessness, youth crime and identity shame. Brokenness in family relationships is a wilderness that is hidden behind closed doors, but God brings transformation as we open up to His healing love.

Jesus told this story because He knew His Father and knew the incredible depths of love constantly flowing from His heart. He also knew His depth of longing for relationship with His children and for them to truly become His beloved and respected heirs.

Jesus' listeners thought of God as Lord and Judge, but He had been Father from the beginning. We see in the Genesis story how He delighted in creating this universe with mankind as the height of His creation. The first thing He did with Adam was to talk with him and draw him into a beautiful partnership as He gave him responsibility to name all that He had created. Yes, Adam and Eve lost that partnership because of their sin, but they never lost God as Father. Throughout the Old Testament story we see Him constantly watching over His children, providing for their needs, loving to be with them, guiding them, grieving over them when they go wrong, angry for a time but loving forever.

Jesus described the father in this story as overwhelmed with joy at the return of his delinquent son. He ran, he kissed, he threw a banquet, he embraced, he gave him a ring, a new robe and shoes. He couldn't lavish enough love on his son.

It is this same love that Father God lavishes on you and me:

"How great is the love the Father has lavished on us, that we should be called children of God. And that is what we are." (1 John 3:1)

Lavish – He loves us without limit. Nothing can separate us from His love for Jesus dealt with that separation for us on the cross, when He endured on our behalf the agony of His Father turning away from Him. We are loved with the same love with which the Father loves Jesus.

As I wrote the above words I saw a picture of someone struggling with an extremely heavy suitcase. You could hardly lift it and were bent over trying to manage it. Father God came to take it from you, saying it was too heavy for you and that it belonged to Him. You were protesting because you believed you could never let go of it – it was part of you. But as He touched the handle, the suitcase fell from your hand without any effort. He opened the lid and there was a momentary glimpse of many, many black weights inside, some small some large. Then, as His light shone in, they disappeared and a moment later the suitcase disappeared too. It was gone and you could stand upright and walk freely. He took your hand, embraced you and began to dance with you.

"The Lord has taken away your punishment ... The Lord your God is with you, He is mighty to save. He will take great delight in you. He will quiet you with His love, He will rejoice over you with singing." (Zephaniah 3:15,17)

Remember, in the story, the younger son returns feeling worthless, but when the father embraces him, he receives his love and goes in to the celebrations, whereas the older son does not.

Reflect

The father in Jesus' parable never stopped loving both his sons, but only one son responded. Your Heavenly Father never gives up loving *you* unconditionally and lavishly. Will you respond to Him?

Prayer

Thank you, my Father, for making me your beloved child. Please help me to respond fully to your love. Amen.

Extra Readings

Hosea 11:1-4; Psalm 68:4-6

Day 40 – The Winter is Past

(Song of Songs 2:10-13)

"My beloved spoke and said to me: 'Arise, my darling, my beautiful one, come with me. See the winter is past...'"

As we reach the end of our sojourn in the wilderness, God wants to fill your heart with hope. In these beautiful verses from the Song of Songs He says,

"See the winter is past, the rains are over and gone. Flowers appear on the earth; the season of singing has come ... Arise, come my darling, my beautiful one, come with me."

It is a heartfelt invitation for us to step into His promise of love and growth. Yes, we may have been trapped in hopelessness, grief, testing, fear... But that was for a season, not forever.

Throughout our time there He has been showing us His deep compassion and the joy He takes in bringing fruit out of the most barren soil. Now He says that, *"the winter is past."* You may feel you are still in Winter, but His word is true. He is calling you to step forward into the promise of Spring.

As I was praying, the Lord spoke to me through a beautiful tree outside my window. The tree was majestic, but it had lost its leaves and had not yet grown new ones. It seemed naked and exposed because its protective covering of leaves was gone.

God said that you have been feeling like that. He created you to reveal His majesty, but something has made you feel exposed and vulnerable – as if you have lost everything that gave your life beauty. God says this is not true, for just as the tree has to experience loss in order to birth its new growth, so He is bringing about a beautiful new growth in you.

In the tree the new leaves are there long before they are actually seen, and in the same way, His new work in your life is there, even though you cannot see it yet. There is no doubt the leaves will come on that tree, and there is no doubt that His new love, beauty and gifts will be born in your life. He says, *"Be at peace, let go of the past and trust that I know how to bring you into that new life."*

How can you let go of the past, that barren place of rejection and loss?

One of the recurring themes we've explored through these forty days is how the Lord loves to speak to us, to cherish and affirm us as His child. He says to us, *"You are altogether beautiful"* when we feel ugly or inferior. Choose to receive the truth of how God sees you. He says, *"There is no flaw in you."* Choose to accept that God has freely forgiven you and you are covered with the purity of His Son.

As we journey out of the wilderness, it's important that we commit ourselves to staying close to Him and listening for His voice. Our hearts need to become soft and responsive to His love. Song of Songs 1:4 says *"draw me after you, let us run together."* That is a beautiful picture of the partnership He longs to develop with us. He promises to always be with us and to turn our mourning into joy.

Reflect

God calls us in Song of Songs 2:14 to come out of our *"hiding places on the mountainside"* because He wants to hear our voice and enjoy the sweetness of our conversation; to see us and be close to us because we are lovely to Him.

As you read those words, release to Him all the ways in which you are still hiding yourself away. Tell Him what's on your heart. Listen for His voice and let Him take your hand and lead you into the Spring.

Extra Readings

Romans 15;13; Luke 7:36-50

A Final Prayer

Father, thank you that you are constantly with me at every stage in my life and never stop loving me.

In those moments when my dreams are shattered and I feel overwhelmed, you are there holding me safe.

Thank you that you are for me, not against me, and in your love you are always working to bring beauty and joy out of my ashes.

Thank you, Lord Jesus, for all you have been showing me of the deep things of your love on this journey through the desert places of my life. Thank you, Holy Spirit, for your ongoing transformation in my life and for enabling me to hear the voice of God and to know God's all surpassing power.

I love you, O Lord my God, and step forward with joy and confidence into all you have for me.

In your precious name, Lord Jesus,

Amen.

About the Author

Tracy Williamson is an author and speaker working together with the blind Gospel Singer, Marilyn Baker for the itinerant music and teaching ministry, MBM Trust www.mbm-ministries.org

Tracy has written several books including: *Expecting God to Speak to You* (New Wine 2004), *Letting God Speak Through You* (New Wine 2005), *Encountering God* (New Wine 2007) and *Flying Free with God* (New Wine 2008). Her latest book *The Father's Kiss* was published by Authentic Media in 2018.

Tracy became deaf and sight/balance impaired at 2 years old when she developed Measles Encephalitis. She had many difficulties in her early years including losing her father to cancer at age 7 and with her hearing loss not being diagnosed till she was 12, facing much misunderstanding and bullying at school. Other deep struggles including abuse and rejection caused Tracy to go into a deep depression in her later teens. Tracy went to college in Herts and ultimately took a BA Hons Degree in English Literature and Education after trying to train for teaching but finding her deafness too much of a struggle. Tracy became a Christian at the end of her 1st year and began a journey into God's Father love that she has been on ever since.

Tracy shares a home with Marilyn and Tracy's Hearing Dog, Goldie, near Tonbridge in Kent. Tracy loves being with friends, worshipping, reading, eating out and enjoying the beauty of creation with her dog!

If you are interested in follwing Tracy or having her speak at your church or group please contact MBM – info@mbm-ministries.org or visit their website or Marilyn Baker Ministries Facebook Page or Tracy Williamson Author Facebook Page.

Recommended Reading

I read constantly so couldn't possibly share a comprehensive list of good books but those listed here are some that have especially blessed me in recent months.

Still Emily by Emily Owen

Catching Contentment by Liz Carter

The Making of Us by Sheridan Voysey

Turning Point by Jennifer Rees Larcombe

Journey Into God's Heart by Jennifer Rees Larcombe

Shattered by Rachel & Tim Wright

The Power of Seven by Emily Owen

Jesus Calling by Sarah Young

Dear Friend 1 & 2 by Vicki Cottingham